THE INNER GAME OF LEADERSHIP
HOW LEADERS CONQUER STRESS TO SHINE IN TURBULENCE

NEURO-RESILIENCE SKILLS
VOLUME 1

PAUL O'NEILL

For Gillian—

whose grace under pressure has taught me more about resilience than any theory ever could.

Your presence has stilled all my storms—and still, my love for you rages on.

And for Carmen—

may you grow up knowing that your infectious joy is your mightiest strength.

You are the rhythm behind every word in these pages.

This book may be about staying grounded—

but you both elevate me every day.

ENDORSEMENTS

"It's rare that I would use such a word but it's extremely well-earned in Paul's case: he is a visionary. His ability to make the complex simple, to get to the heart of an issue and to recommend an effective solution is outstanding. His vitality and energy is infectious"

Emma Jensen, Vice President, Small Business, OPTUS

"Through the lens of research in neuroscience, Paul can forge interventions that promote resilience. His type of coaching allowed me to be better equipped to cope with stress and adversity, at my level, but also recognising the signs in other people and helped me being a better manager"

Jessica Scalzo, Variety Improvement Manager, COSTA

"Paul is one of the energizing and gifted leaders I know. He is also one of the most skilled NLP practitioners I have had the good fortune to meet"

Tim Dalmau, CEO, Dalmau Consulting

"As a leader, Paul has a unique quality rarely seen in today's leaders and that is: the ability to find and bring out 'the best' in people"

Tony Enache, CFO, Farm Pride Foods.

"Paul offers a refreshing take on leadership and workplace change strategies. He provides time efficient tailored insights and solutions to support and equip leaders to develop, reframe perspectives and shift the status quo to deliver positive outcomes suited to today's dynamic work environment"

Elizabeth Brockbank, Environmental Manager, ALCOA

"Paul demonstrated a balanced consultative senior management approach that could quickly interpret and translate detailed plans and how they could consolidate into overall strategies for KPI success"

Peter Sheehan, Director GM, Western Sydney Airport.

"Paul is an excellent trainer who has transformed my life. His amazing skills, dedicated care and consistent emotional intelligence has opened a new world for me to view"

Philip Hoang, Data Engineer, CBHS

"Paul has been an invaluable asset to both myself personally and in my business strategies. Paul and his unique skill set have aided constant changes in the business and personal arena that mean I achieved positive rather than negative outcomes personally and financially"

Ben Kavich, Director, Workhorse Group of Companies

"My life was just like 'work-retire-die'. But this has changed dramatically after I had couple of sessions with Paul. With his help, I can recognise myself, again. I learned to love myself and make myself a priority, again. Paul's training has not only changed my life, it changed my whole family's life"

Iris Huangfu, Accountant, Sydney, Australia

"Paul's intervention and guidance was a game changer. It's not easy to put into words the impact that his NLP practice had as it wasn't singular nor limited to just myself or to that point in time. Personally, I was brought back to a feeling of inner strength and reminded, not through words or description, but through creating an experience, that I can be in control of how I feel and create calm from within my own skin"

V. Madsen, Perth, Australia.

"I would like to thank Paul for transforming my life. He helped me find a completely different mindset, which you will find will help you discover the keys to the life that you deserve, too. As a female going through the beginnings of divorce, it has not been easy. But I have now gained a deep sense of security and confidence. And I have the excitement of a wonderful new future"

L. Diaz, Sydney, NSW.

"Paul is a fantastic hypnotist who has helped me with a lot of my deep personal issues, both for work and my private life. Every time, he works his magic. Truly, he is simply the best!"

A. Gonzales, Registered Nurse, Sydney, Australia.

"The tools / techniques I learnt through my time with Paul will stay with me a lifetime, and why wouldn't I want that when I'm feeling like I'm floating in champagne bubbles"

Jacqueline D., Palates Instructor, Queensland, Australia

CONTENTS

Preface   xi

PART ONE
INSTINCTUAL FOUNDATIONS

Introduction   3
1. Instinctual Contact   7
2. Instinctual Awareness   13
3. Instinctual Acuity   25
   Section One Summary   39

PART TWO
PERSONAL RESILIENCE SKILLS

Introduction   55
4. Core Skills   59
5. Intermediate Skills   69
6. Advanced Skills   81
   Section Two Summary   91

PART THREE
REPAIR & PREVENT TRAUMA

Introduction   109
7. When Safety is Ruptured   113
8. Rupture Repair Coaching   123
9. Rupture Prevention   149
   Section Three Summary   169

Conclusion	175
Afterword	193
Notes	197
Bibliography	201
Index	205
Acknowledgments	207
About the Author	209
Also by Paul O'Neill	211

PREFACE

They never tell you this at the start: leadership doesn't begin in the boardroom. It begins in the gut, when the pressure hits and your hands tremble slightly and the clock ticks louder than it should. It begins before you speak, before you plan, before you even act. It begins with what you do the moment your body feels like running—and you choose not to.

For all the talk of strategy and vision, what breaks most leaders isn't the task. It's the weight. The pressure of uncertainty. The unrelenting demands to decide faster, speak clearer, and hold steady while others fracture. We don't rise to the level of our training in those moments. We sink to the level of our self-command.

And yet, most leaders are taught to suppress that part of themselves—the breath, the instinct, the flicker of emotion in the spine. They've been told to outthink their fear. To control their stress with sheer will. To grit through. But gritting is not the same as grounding. And willpower is no substitute for true mastery.

This book is for the leader who senses there's more to it than muscling through. Who's felt the disconnect between what they know and what they do. Who's walked out of a high-stakes meeting thinking, 'I had the words, but I didn't have myself.'

The inner game is not about fixing your flaws. It's about learning to stay with yourself in real time. To notice the physiological wave before it becomes panic. To remain present, not performative. To respond from choice, not compulsion. This is where real authority begins—not the power to control others, but the capacity to regulate your own state when it matters most.

Inside these pages, you'll find tools forged not in theory but in lived tension. Techniques I've tested in boardrooms, crisis briefings, and quiet moments before difficult conversations. You'll learn methods like the *Tension Releasor*—a rapid state reset for when the walls close in. Or *Dual-Mind Reflection*, which helps you decode the subtle war between what you feel and what you believe. These aren't rituals. They're real-time practices. They're anchors.

But more than tools, I hope this book offers you something else— permission. Permission to feel without losing control. Permission to take your cues from the body as well as the brief. Permission to meet yourself at the level where leadership actually begins.

Because it doesn't begin when you issue orders, or map a vision. It begins when you walk into the room and change the temperature without saying a word. When people feel safer just because you're there. When your presence slows the chaos, not just for you, but for everyone else.

This is not an abstract promise. It's a trained capacity. And it's not beyond you. In fact, it's already within you—visible in moments of quiet decisiveness, calm defiance, silent composure. My job is simply to help you access it more reliably.

So take a breath. Not a metaphorical one—a real breath. Because this journey doesn't start with grand ideas. It starts with what you do in the seconds between stimulus and response.

The rest of your leadership unfolds from there.

Paul O'Neill

November 2024

PART ONE
INSTINCTUAL FOUNDATIONS

INTRODUCTION

*And when everyone's screaming,
nobody hears the truth*
George Orwell

Leadership is often depicted as a cerebral endeavour, demanding strategic thinking, clear decision-making, and logical precision. Yet beneath the veneer of calculated reasoning lies a primal force that shapes our choices more than we realise: instinct. The *Instinctual Foundations* part of 'The Inner Game' invites readers to explore this hidden dimension of leadership, where ancient neural pathways and gut-level reactions coalesce with current challenges. Through three chapters—*Instinctual Contact, Instinctual Awareness,* and *Instinctual Acuity*—this part offers an illuminating journey into the unconscious drivers of decision-making, helping leaders refine their instincts for better outcomes.

Human instincts, developed through millennia of survival, are as relevant in the boardroom as they were on the savannah. Consider the snap of a twig in a dark forest: your heart races, muscles tense, and senses sharpen, ready for fight, flight, or freeze. This primal response, orchestrated by the ancient structures of the brain, serves as a compass during moments of uncertainty and potential threat. In our time, however, this same mechanism often misfires, interpreting subtle workplace tensions as life-or-death scenarios. Leaders must therefore learn not only to understand these instincts but to master them.

Chapter 1, *Instinctual Contact*, begins with an exploration of our "gut feelings"—those visceral reactions that guide decisions before conscious thought intervenes. From the immediate physiological effects of stress to the intricate dialogue between the gut and the brain, this chapter unravels the neuroscience behind instinct. It introduces techniques like the *Tension Releasor*, a practice designed to ground leaders in moments of pressure by fostering a state of metabolic congruence. By understanding how instinct manifests in physical sensations, leaders can develop a keener sense of when to trust their gut and when to question it.

In Chapter 2, *Instinctual Awareness*, the focus shifts to the *Triune Brain Theory*, a model that illuminates the interplay between our instinctual, emotional, and rational minds. While neuroscience highlights the interconnectedness of brain functions, the *Triune Brain* provides a practical framework for understanding leadership behaviours. The *Reptilian Brain* governs survival instincts, the *Mammalian Brain* navigates social connections, and the *Primate Brain* enables strategic thinking. This chapter explores how these layers interact in high-stakes scenarios, offering exercises like the *Dual-Mind Reflection* to help leaders balance gut reactions with rational analysis.

The final chapter, *Instinctual Acuity*, delves deeper into the unconscious processes that guide our decisions. Drawing on the concept of *neuroception*—our nervous system's ability to detect safety or danger without conscious awareness—it reveals how leaders can hone their instincts for greater precision. Techniques such as *The Worry*

Solver and *Connect with Yourself* help leaders transform stress into clarity, tapping into their "Unconscious Navigator" for more effective decision-making. Through case stories, such as contrasting leadership styles of risk-averse and bold decision-makers, this chapter illustrates how instinct can be both a strength and a liability.

Collectively, these chapters offer more than just theoretical insights. They provide practical tools and exercises to help leaders engage with their instincts, build resilience, and navigate the complexities of modern leadership. By increasing their instinct awareness, refining their unconscious patterns, and balancing primal impulses with deliberate reasoning, leaders can unlock a deeper level of personal and professional mastery.

The *Instinctual Foundations* part is a call to action for leaders to embrace the wisdom of their bodies and minds. It challenges the dichotomy between reason and intuition, offering a pathway to integrate the two. In doing so, it equips leaders not only to survive in the high-pressure environments of today's world but to thrive—leading with clarity, confidence and congruence.

ONE
INSTINCTUAL CONTACT

Fear, relentless and inescapable,
fastens upon the hearts of men.
Homer

YOU ARE VENTURING through a dense woodland with your family as twilight descends. The air is crisp, and the forest hums with the subtle rustling of leaves and the distant calls of unseen creatures. Suddenly, the snap of a twig echoes nearby. Instinctively, your heart quickens, muscles tense, and senses sharpen. Without conscious deliberation, you're poised to react—fight, flight or freeze. This immediate, instinctual response emanates from a deep-seated part of us often referred to as the "Gut"[1]. It's a primal compass, honed over millennia, guiding us through moments of uncertainty and potential danger.

In the realm of leadership, this primal instinct plays a pivotal role, influencing decisions and actions in ways we might not fully comprehend. Our 'gut reactions', rooted in the ancient structures of the brain and influenced by unconscious non-verbal cues, are ever-present forces shaping our leadership styles and organisational cultures. Understanding the influence of 'the gut' is essential for navigating the complexities of today's leadership, where swift judgement, adaptability, and emotional intelligence can make the difference between success and failure.

Consider the case of Sharon, a seasoned CEO facing a critical decision about a potential merger. The numbers look promising, the market analysts are optimistic, and her team is enthusiastic. Yet, as she sits in the boardroom, poised to sign the agreement, a nagging feeling in her stomach gives her pause. Something doesn't feel right. In that moment, Sharon faces a quintessential leadership dilemma: should she trust her gut instinct or proceed based on the rational analysis before her?

This scenario illustrates the double-edged nature of instinct in leadership. On one hand, Sharon's gut feeling could be drawing on years of experience and subconscious pattern recognition, alerting her to subtle red flags that her conscious mind hasn't yet processed. On the other hand, it could be an irrational fear response, perhaps triggered by a past negative experience that bears no relevance to the current situation. The challenge for Sharon, as for all leaders, lies in discerning when to heed these instinctual warnings and when to override them.

The concept of "gut feeling" is more than just a convenient metaphor. Recent advances in neuroscience have revealed a complex network of neurons lining our digestive tract, often referred to as the "second brain"[2]. This *enteric nervous system* communicates bidirectionally with our central nervous system, influencing and being influenced by our emotional states and cognitive processes. When we speak of having a "gut reaction", we're acknowledging a very real physiological phenomenon—one that has profound implications for how we make decisions, especially under pressure.

. . .

Somatic Honing

> *The conscious mind may be compared to a fountain playing in the sun and falling back into the great subterranean pool of subconscious from which it rises*[3]
> **Sigmund Freud**

Let us embark on an exploration of instinct and awareness, a practice designed to help leaders tune into and achieve increased awareness of their physical sensations. In particular, those subtle signals that so often go unnoticed (or we choose to ignore) but can shape our decision-making in profound ways[4]. This exercise is about cultivating a sharper awareness of your body's responses—responses that, if listened to, can ground your thinking and sharpen your instincts.

Start by finding a quiet space where you won't be disturbed. Sit or lie down, whichever is most comfortable for you. This practice works best when you are completely at ease, allowing your attention to gently turn inward.

Begin by focusing on your breath. Take a slow, deep inhale through your nose, and then exhale through your mouth. Repeat this a few times. There is nothing complicated about this; it's simply a way to settle your mind, to remind your body that it can relax into the moment. Feel the rhythm of your breathing, and let it become an *anchor* for your attention.

Now, let's shift your focus to your toes. Bring your awareness there, as though you are scanning them with the light of your attention. What do you notice? Is there tension, warmth, or perhaps a neutral stillness? The key here is not to change anything, but to observe. Let your body reveal its sensations to you without any interference.

Gradually, move your attention upwards. Slowly, methodically, focus on your feet, ankles, calves, knees, and thighs. As you bring awareness

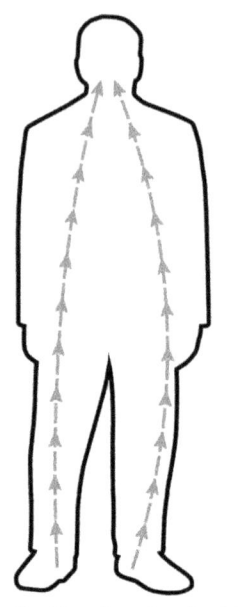

Somatic Honing Body Map

to each area, you may notice certain sensations—tension, comfort, even a subtle vibration. Observe these sensations as though you are an explorer, encountering them for the first time. There's no need to analyse or react, simply allow your awareness to pass through, like a gentle breeze.

As you continue upward, pay close attention to your abdomen and chest. This is often where your gut instincts live, where emotional responses can manifest as tightness, discomfort, or a sense of ease. Take your time here. What does your gut feel like in this moment? Is it calm? Is it tense? Simply notice without judgment. This is where much of our intuitive intelligence resides, often giving us subtle hints before our conscious mind catches up.

Next, bring your focus to your shoulders, neck, and head. These areas tend to be reservoirs for stress. Scan through them carefully, noticing if there is tightness in your neck, tension in your jaw, or pressure in your temples. Again, observe without trying to force anything to change.

Once you've completed this body scan, return to your breath. Take several deep, calming breaths, and with each exhale, let go of any residual tension you may still feel. Focus on the areas that stood out the most during your scan—the ones that felt tight or uncomfortable. As you exhale, imagine that tension gently dissolving.

Now, reflect for a moment. What did you learn from this process? Did you notice any signals—perhaps from your gut or areas of tension—that might be speaking to you about something in your life? This awareness is not just a passive observation; it is a tool you can carry forward. When making decisions, return to this feeling. Ask yourself, *"What is my body telling me?"*

This practice is not just about calming the mind, though that is a natural by-product. It's about fostering a more intimate relationship with your own internal signals, the subtle cues that often guide us when we listen. By increasing your instinct awareness, you'll find yourself making decisions that are more grounded, more intuitive, and more in tune with your deeper sense of knowing.

In time, this connection with your physical self becomes second nature, offering a source of clarity and insight that enhances your leadership and personal growth.

As we delve deeper into the neurological underpinnings of leadership instinct, we'll explore how this ancient compass within us operates in the boardrooms, team dynamics, and organisational challenges of our current era. We'll unravel the complex interplay between our reptilian instincts, our mammalian emotions, and our higher cognitive functions. Through this journey, we aim to equip leaders with a deeper understanding of their internal processes[5], enabling them to harness the power of instinct while mitigating its potential pitfalls.

In the chapters that follow, we'll embark on a fascinating exploration of the neuroscience behind instinct, examining how our brains process information and make split-second decisions. We'll investigate the role of non-verbal communication in triggering instinctual responses, and how these subtle cues can ripple through an organisation, shaping its culture and performance. We'll delve into the concept of the collective reptilian brain, understanding how instincts can spread through a group, sometimes leading to innovative breakthroughs, and other times to destructive groupthink.

Crucially, we'll also explore the vital role of psychological safety in leadership, understanding how leaders can create environments that allow for healthy expression and modulation of instinctual responses. We'll introduce the concept of neuro-resilience, a set of skills that leaders can develop to better navigate the often-turbulent waters of instinct-driven decision making.

As we progress, we'll grapple with the leader's dilemma—how to balance the often-contradictory pulls of instinct, emotion, and reason. Through case stories and practical exercises, we'll provide leaders with tools to refine their instincts, making them more reliable guides in complex and chaotic situations.

Our journey through the realm of gut instinct in leadership promises to be as challenging as it is enlightening. By the end, we hope to have provided a comprehensive map of this internal terrain, enabling leaders to navigate with greater confidence and skill. After all, in the fast-paced, ever-shifting sands of leadership at this time, our ancient instincts may well be our most valuable compass—if we learn to read them correctly.

TWO
INSTINCTUAL AWARENESS

To know thyself is the beginning of wisdom
Socrates

GUT INSTINCTS often guide our leadership decisions. To understand them, we must first embark on a journey into the intricate workings of the human brain. Our destination? The ancient neural structures that have been shaping our responses to the world long before we developed the capacity for complex thought.

The *Triune Brain Theory*[1], first proposed by neuroscientist Paul D. MacLean in the 1960s, offers a compelling framework for understanding the evolutionary layers of our brain and how they influence our behaviour. While neuroscience has revealed that brain function is more interconnected than this model suggests, however, the Triune Brain remains a useful tool for thinking about the brain's core functions. Just as Newtonian physics is sufficient for most non-physicists, unless you need to delve into Einstein's theories, the Triune Brain provides a practical way for leaders to understand how instinct, emotion, and reason shape our responses in leadership contexts.

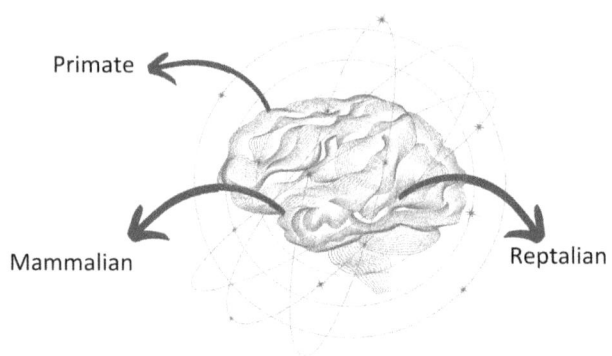

Think of our brain as a city built and rebuilt over millennia. At its core lies the old town, with narrow, winding streets and ancient structures—this is our *Reptilian Brain*[2]. Surrounding it is a bustling medieval quarter, filled with the hustle and bustle of emotion and social connection—our *Mammalian Brain*. Finally, enveloping it all is a futuristic metropolis of towering skyscrapers, representing our *Primate Brain*, capable of abstract thought and complex problem-solving. Now, let's take a closer look at each of these "districts" in our neural city:

Primal Puppet Master

At the base of our brain, sitting atop the spinal column, lies the most ancient part of our neural architecture—the *Reptilian Brain*. This includes structures like the brainstem and cerebellum, which govern our most basic survival functions. Think of it as the ever-vigilant night watchman of our neural city, constantly scanning for threats.

The Reptilian Brain is responsible for our most instinctual responses: fight, flight or freeze[3]. It's the part of us that reacts before we have time to think, the source of that gut feeling that something isn't quite right[4]. In leadership contexts, this part of our brain might cause us to bristle at a perceived challenge to our authority or instinctively back away from a risky proposition.

Looping back to Sharon, our CEO facing a crucial merger decision:

As she sits in the boardroom, her Reptilian Brain *is scanning the environment, picking up on subtle cues—like the tension in a colleague's voice or the slight shift in another's body language. These signals are processed below her conscious awareness. However, even though she is not consciously aware that they are happening, their affect is still contributing to that uneasy feeling in her stomach. While the Reptilian Brain's immediate responses can be lifesaving in truly dangerous situations, because they are a binary light-switch, not an analogue dimmer-switch, they can lead us astray in much more nuanced contexts of progressive leadership, where 'threats' are more 'concerns', requiring more subtle and require nuanced responses.*

As Sharon is in a fight-flight mode, not a calm social engagement mode, her metabolism is out of sync with her environment. The first part of being congruent when engaging with stakeholders, is to be metabolically congruent with the environment in which you engage them. That requires that you engage with yourself to begin with. Once you feel grounded and centred, your metabolic, emotional and behavioural responses will pivot into your social engagement mode, naturally and without volition.

TENSION RELEASOR

With that in mind, let's turn our attention to a practice that offers a gentle yet effective way to soothe the mind and body quickly—a practice rooted in self-awareness and soft, deliberate action. The goal here is not only to relax but also to engage in a quiet dialogue with yourself, inviting deeper awareness into how you carry tension and how you can let it go.

I call this technique the *Tension Releasor* because stress builds tension in one's body and it stays there until it is released. Going on holiday, having a massage, making love and a relaxing in a nice warm bath will all release tension. However, such activities tend not to be available whilst at work, which is where this technique comes, requiring just fifteen-twenty minutes, initially. With practice, you'll be able to get the same affect under five minutes, even as you in the middle of a meeting with your eyes wide open.

Begin by settling into a comfortable position, preferably somewhere you won't be disturbed directly – there may well be ambient noise but that's alright. If you're ready, gently close your eyes and take a moment to acknowledge how you feel right now. Notice any tension, whether it's in your body or mind. This simple act of recognition is the first step—it's as if you're introducing yourself to the feeling, making it less elusive.

Now, hear a calm, kind voice in your mind. It's your voice, but gentler, quieter. This voice is going to guide you through the next few moments. The tone is important—it's somewhere between a loving command and a gentle suggestion, it's a warm invitation for your body to let go of any tension it doesn't need anymore.

You're encouraging yourself to soften, to relax, but you're doing it in a way that feels effortless, as if you're gently coaxing your body and mind into a calmer state. We'll begin at the top of your head and slowly move down through your body. As we move through each

INSTINCTUAL AWARENESS

part, focus your awareness there, and if you find tension, picture that area being softly massaged, the way a skilled hand might ease out a knot. Before you begin, read and fully understand the instructions. In support, a short form version of the exercise is in the end of this part.

Start with your head and, ever so gently, ever so softly, say:

- *"My scalp can soften and relax now..."*
- *"My eyes can soften and relax now..."*
- *"My mouth can soften and relax now..."*
- *"My tongue can soften and relax now..."*
- *"My jaw can soften and relax now..."*

Feel each area gently yielding, as if tension is dissolving with each word.

Now, let's move to your neck, shoulders, and arms. This area often holds more strain than we realise:

- *"My neck can soften and relax now..."*
- *"My shoulders can soften and relax now..."*
- *"My arms can soften and relax now..."*
- *"My hands can soften and relax now..."*

Imagine that tension slipping away, your muscles becoming lighter, looser.

Next, we focus on the back and the muscles that support your posture:

- *"My upper back can soften and relax now..."*
- *"My lower back can soften and relax now..."*
- *"My glutes can soften and relax now..."*

Here, picture the tension evaporating from you, like steam from a coffee cup.

And finally, bring your awareness to your legs and feet, grounding your relaxation:

- *"My thighs can soften and relax now..."*
- *"My calves can soften and relax now..."*
- *"My feet can soften and relax now..."*

As you move through each part of your body, feel the subtle shift, the softening that comes with attention and suggestion.

Now, allow your awareness to rest on your mind itself:

- *"And now, my mind can soften and relax more and more..."*

Let this be a moment of surrender, as if your mind is letting go of what it used to 'need' to hold onto and now is a choice to let go.

Pause here for a while. Simply notice how you feel. You might find that you're more relaxed than when you began. You can stay in this feeling for as long as you like, and if you wish, you can repeat the process, perhaps finding new areas that need softening.

When you're ready to return to full awareness, know that you'll feel refreshed, clear, and alert, as though this moment of calm has gently reset your mind and body. In practising this, you're not just releasing tension—you're cultivating a deeper connection with your own capacity for peace, a resource you can return to again and again.

This is the art of *softening*, and in mastering it, you'll discover how to ease the everyday tensions that life brings while opening yourself to a deeper relationship with your own inner self; as well as, for leadership purposes, your sense of centredness will translate into non-verbal congruence.

Emotional Compass

Encircling our reptilian core is the *Mammalian Brain*, also known as the limbic system. This is the realm of emotion, motivation, and social bonding. If the Reptilian Brain is our night watchman, the Mammalian Brain is our social secretary, constantly navigating the complex web of relationships and emotional cues that define our social world.

Key structures in the Mammalian Brain include the amygdala, which processes emotions like fear, and the hippocampus, crucial for memory formation. This part of our brain allows us to form attachments, feel empathy, and navigate social hierarchies—all vital skills for effective leadership.

In our neural city metaphor, the Mammalian Brain is where social life thrives—in bustling markets and cozy taverns, where alliances are formed, trust is built, and emotional intelligence is developed.

For Sharon, her Mammalian Brain allows her to read the room, sensing excitement or apprehension from her team members. It helps her form bonds with colleagues, inspiring loyalty and commitment. However, it can also introduce biases, such as instinctively trusting someone who reminds her of a mentor or distrusting someone based on past experiences.

The *Mammalian Brain* adds complexity to our instinctual responses. It's not just about survival but about thriving in a social context. This can lead to more sophisticated gut reactions, like "This person feels trustworthy" or "This deal feels right."

Reason & Foresight

> *We can be blind to the obvious,*
> *and we are also blind to our blindness.*
> **Daniel Kahneman**

Finally, we come to the most recent addition to our neural architecture—the *Primate Brain*, primarily comprising the neocortex. This part of the brain distinguishes humans (and other primates) from most mammals, enabling our highest cognitive functions: abstract thinking, language, planning and consciousness itself[5]. In our neural city, the Primate Brain is the gleaming financial district, where complex deals are struck, and innovation happens. It gives us the ability to step back, see the bigger picture, and weigh the pros and cons of a decision with logical precision.

But here's the paradox: even as our Primate Brain enables careful, rational thought, it doesn't operate in isolation. Beneath the surface, the older systems of our brain—our emotional Mammalian Brain and instinct-driven Reptilian Brain—are constantly influencing our decisions. This interplay between instinct and reason is what Daniel Kahneman famously described in, *'Thinking, Fast and Slow'* as the tension between *System 1*, our fast, automatic, and intuitive mode of thinking, and *System 2*, our slow, deliberate, and analytical mode.

As leaders, understanding how these three layers of the brain interact is crucial. In high-pressure, high-stakes situations—like responding to a crisis—we may need to rely on the quick, instinctual reactions of our Reptilian Brain. But for long-term strategic planning, our Primate Brain's capacity for abstract thought is essential. And yet, in the most pivotal moments, neither can act alone. Great leadership isn't about choosing one over the other—it's about integrating these different brain functions into a cohesive decision-making process.

This means learning to respect the speed and efficiency of our instinctual reactions while tempering them with the clarity and depth of rational analysis. Kahneman's work reminds us that both systems have their strengths: instinct can guide us toward insights we might otherwise overlook, while reason ensures we don't fall prey to biases or emotional impulses.

Now suppose you're facing an important decision—one of those moments when the pressure is on, and your instinct is to act quickly. This is where the balance of these two systems becomes critical. Instead of rushing, I want you to consider the value of a pause. This pause isn't just about slowing down; it's about creating a moment of reflection to access the strengths of both systems.

What we're going to explore is a technique I like to call the *Dual-Mind Reflection*. It's a structured way to engage both your rational mind and your instinctive gut feelings before making any major decision. Let's walk through it step by step, and you'll see how this process can help you navigate those critical moments with more clarity and balance.

DUAL-MIND REFLECTION

The first step is surprisingly simple yet often overlooked: *acknowledge the decision point*. You need to consciously recognise that you're about to make a choice. It sounds obvious, but by merely acknowledging it, you're already shifting from a reactive mode—where you might be driven by urgency or impulse—into a more reflective, deliberate state. This awareness is crucial because it sets the stage for everything that follows.

Now, once you've recognised the decision, I want you to take a deep breath—but don't underestimate the power of this breath. This isn't just a casual inhale; it's a signal to your body and mind that you're taking a moment to pause. A deep breath helps to disengage any immediate emotional reactions that might cloud your judgment. It gives you space, a bit of room to think.

Next, let's *engage the 4-7-8 Breathing Technique*. It's simple but remarkably effective at calming the nervous system and clearing the mind. Here's how it works: inhale through your nose for a count of four seconds. Hold that breath for seven seconds. Then, exhale slowly through your mouth for eight seconds. Do these three or four times. What this does, physiologically, is slow down your heart rate and give your brain a chance to shift out of its reactive state and into a more reflective one.

Once you've calmed your body, it's time to focus on the *rational aspects of the decision*. What are the facts? What do you know for sure? What are the pros and cons? This is the moment to engage your analytical mind. Look at the data. Examine the situation logically. Ask yourself: what does the evidence say? This step is all about detaching from any emotional noise and seeing the decision through a purely rational lens.

But we're not stopping there, because decisions aren't made in a vacuum of pure logic. Now I want you to *shift your attention to your gut feelings*. How does this decision make you feel? Beyond the facts and figures, there's often a more visceral reaction we have to major decisions. Do you feel a sense of excitement? Maybe hesitation or discomfort? These feelings are important. They're not just background noise—they're your body and mind giving you subtle feedback that might not show up in your rational analysis. So, take a moment to honour those feelings, whatever they may be.

At this point, you're going to *scan your body for any physical sensations*. Pay attention to areas like your gut, your chest, your shoulders. Is there tension? Are there any tight spots? Often, your body will reveal stress or unease before you're fully conscious of it. These sensations can be clues about how you really feel about the decision, even if your mind hasn't quite caught up yet.

Now comes the interesting part: *balancing the two perspectives*. You've looked at the rational side, and you've explored your gut instincts. Are they aligned? Do they point in the same direction, or are they pulling you apart? This is the moment of synthesis, where you take stock of the full picture. If the rational and instinctual sides agree, great—you've got a clear path forward. If they don't, that's okay too. It means there's more to consider, and that's precisely what this check-in is designed to reveal.

Finally, once you've given space to both your reason and your instinct, it's time to *proceed with your decision*. The point of this exercise isn't to second-guess yourself endlessly, but to pause just long enough to gain a fuller understanding of what's really going on—both in your head and in your gut. By taking this pause, you can move forward with a greater sense of confidence, knowing that you've considered both the logical facts and the emotional insights.

This process, the *Dual-Mind Reflection*, isn't about choosing between logic and intuition. It's about recognising that both play a role in our decision-making, and the best choices are often those that incorporate both. By practising this, especially under pressure, you'll develop a more nuanced, thoughtful approach to leadership—one that's both rational and deeply attuned to your own inner signals.

As you continue to explore your instinctual patterns, ask yourself:

- *"When have I overridden a gut instinct in favour of rational thought?*
- *Did it lead to a better outcome, or were there unforeseen consequences?"*

CONVERSELY:

- *"Have there been times when trusting my instincts led me to success?"*

These reflections will help you hone the balance between intuition and logic, ultimately strengthening your leadership effectiveness.

THREE
INSTINCTUAL ACUITY

*There is more wisdom in your body
than in your deepest philosophies*
Friedrich Nietzsche

NEUROLOGICAL UNDERPINNINGS of our instinctual responses now explored, we now turn our attention to how these ancient systems operate in the current spheres of leadership. Our focus shifts to what we might call the "Unconscious Navigator" - the part of our mind that guides our actions and decisions below the threshold of conscious awareness.

Always On, Always Alert

Recall our earlier metaphor of the brain as a city, with the *Reptilian Brain* serving as the vigilant night watchman. This primordial part of our neural architecture never sleeps, constantly scanning our environment for potential threats or opportunities. In leadership contexts, this translates to an ever-present undercurrent of instinctual responses that can significantly influence our behaviour and decision-making.

Consider our CEO, Sharon, in a highly tense negotiation. While her *Primate Brain* is occupied with the complex details of the deal, her *Reptilian Brain* is ceaselessly monitoring the room. It's attuned to subtle shifts in tone, tiny changes in body language, and barely perceptible alterations in the emotional atmosphere. This unconscious vigilance can manifest as seemingly inexplicable hunches or gut feelings.

For instance, Sharon might suddenly feel a need to change her approach, even though she can't articulate why. Perhaps her *Reptilian Brain* has detected a slight tensing in the jaw of her counterpart, signalling growing resistance that hasn't yet been verbally expressed. This instinctual nudge, if heeded, could lead Sharon to adjust her strategy before the negotiation reaches an impasse.

However, the always-on nature of this system can also lead to false alarms. In our ancestral environment, it was better to overreact to a potential threat than to under-react. But in the corporate environment of this era, this hair-trigger response system can sometimes lead us astray, causing us to react defensively to situations that don't actually pose a threat.

The Body's Threat Detection System

Central to understanding our *Unconscious Navigator* is the concept of *neuroception*[1], a term coined by Stephen Porges as part of his *Polyvagal Theory*. Neuroception refers to our nervous system's ability to detect safety or danger in our environment without conscious awareness.

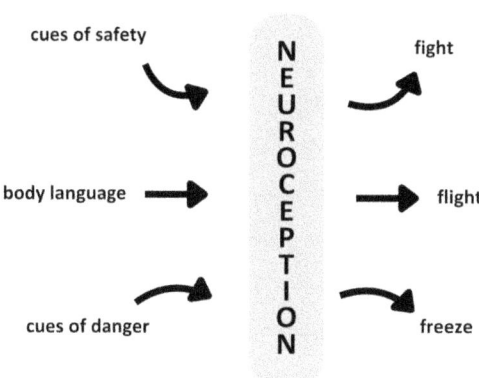

Polyvagal Theory: Reaction Function

This subconscious threat detection system is remarkably sophisticated. It doesn't just respond to obvious dangers, but also to subtle cues that might indicate a shift in the social environment. For a leader, this could mean unconsciously picking up on signs of disengagement in a team meeting, sensing growing tension between colleagues, or feeling a nascent opportunity emerging in a casual conversation.

Let's return to Sharon for an illustration. She's giving a presentation to potential investors. Midway through, she finds herself inexplicably stumbling over her words and feeling a creeping sense of unease. Unbeknownst to her conscious mind, her neuroception has detected signs of scepticism in her audience - perhaps a pattern of crossed arms, averted gazes, or subtle head shakes. Whatever it is, her body is reacting to this perceived threat before her conscious mind has had a chance to process it.

This unconscious threat detection can be incredibly valuable, allowing leaders to respond to situations even before they've fully understood them consciously. However, it can also be misleading if not balanced with conscious reflection. A leader's neuroception might be oversensitive due to past experiences, leading them to perceive threats where none exist. Part and parcel of this aspect is our ability to develop a worry habit.

Let's explore a way to transform worry into something useful and productive—a practice I call *The Worry Solver*. This process invites you to engage with your concerns in a way that turns them from burdens into opportunities for clarity and control.

THE WORRY SOLVER[2]

Start by bringing to mind something that's been causing you concern. This might be a small worry or something that has been looming large in your thoughts. Don't rush through this step; take a moment to really notice what's been on your mind. Acknowledge the worry for what it is—a persistent thought, trying to capture your attention.

Now, ask yourself a simple yet profound question:

"What is the underlying purpose of this worry?

Consider this carefully. As I say to my clients:

"The body complains. It doesn't explain. It leaves that to the brain; and the brain most often get it wrong"[3].

Worry, as frustrating as it can be, often has a 'hidden' purpose. This purpose is hidden because it is often buried somewhere in the *subconscious*; which, as the name implies, is below our conscious awareness.

For example, your body might be trying to protect you. Stephen Porges tells the story about a Fire Chief who called his team to evacuate a building moments before the floor collapsed. He had no cognitive understanding, but he trusted his neuroception's unconscious ability to sense danger. In doing so, he saved himself and his team[4].

Alternatively, your body maybe attempting to prepare you for something. Perhaps there's a big event coming up – a major presentation, a meeting with a disgruntled key client or even a big trip that needs to go well.

There's a phenomenon that I call the *Weekly Worry Pattern*. This is a 'pattern of protection' where the human body is readying itself for danger or threat. It often besets leaders and managers on a Sunday evening, typically any time from 3pm. The bad feelings cause them to scan their work week to find all the likely suspects to explain why they are feeling bad. They then brood, mull and get worked up over all imaginary events that were not bothering them at all at 2pm.

This is a great example of the body complaining and the brain getting it all wrong. There's a better way: If you find yourself worrying, just take a moment and get centred. Perhaps do the *4-7-8 Breathing Technique* and/ or the *Tension Releaser*. Whatever works best for you, once your rational *Primate Brain* is back online, ask yourself:

"How is this worry trying to help me? What does it provide or protect me from?"

You may find that the answer is something related to feeling safe, avoiding risk, or safeguarding a certain outcome. Whatever the reason, it's important to recognise that your worry has a <u>*purpose*</u>, even if it's not serving you in the best way right now.

Once you've identified the reason that resonates with you, it's time to challenge the worry. Here's where we shift from concern to creativity. Ask your mind to come up with at least three different ways to achieve that same positive outcome, but without the stress and discomfort that worrying brings. These new methods should feel like genuine alternatives, ways to keep you safe, prepared, or in control, but in a calmer, more effective manner.

Take a moment to really explore these new options. Do they feel right to you? Does each one offer a solution that brings the same benefits as worrying, but without the emotional toll? If you feel any reluctance or hesitation, pause and ask your mind to resolve any inner disagreements. It's important that you feel at ease with these new approaches, and you'll know you're ready to move forward when you feel a sense of peace and confidence about them.

Now, let's take it a step further. Visualise yourself applying these new strategies in the future. Picture how you might handle similar situations using these calmer, more effective methods. See it, feel it, experience it as though it's already happening. The more you envision this, the more natural it will feel, as though it's the way you've always handled things.

In practising *The Worry Solver*, you're not just managing worry—you're rewiring your response to it. You're training your mind to find solutions that offer the same protection, but with less strain. Over time, this practice will allow you to face life's challenges with a sense of calm confidence, knowing that you have the tools to handle whatever comes your way.

Case Stories

The way our unconscious navigator guides us can vary significantly from one leader to another, shaped by individual experiences, cultural background, and personal temperament. Let's explore the contrasting styles of two brothers, who own and run several small-to-medium sized businesses together.

When the *Reptile* Dominates

Meet Mick, known for his cautious, discipled and methodical approach to business. His leadership style is characterised by a strong aversion to risk, a preference for established procedures, and a tendency to react defensively to new ideas or challenges to the status quo.

We can perceive his leadership style is influenced from an overactive *Reptilian Brain*, due to past experiences of failure, paternal and fraternal conflict in business contexts. Mick's neuroception is hyper-tuned to potential threats, causing him to perceive danger in situations that others might see as opportunities. He uses the word 'No' every time he hears a new idea in order to feel safe.

While this cautious approach can protect the company from certain types of risks, it has also stifled innovation and growth. Mick's team often feel discouraged from presenting new ideas, knowing they're likely to get a 'No' response. Over time, this has led to a stagnant company culture and missed opportunities in the market. In addition, Mick's fight-flight response kicks in immediately after any aspect of his life veers off its prescribed path. His demeanour becomes gruff and surly, treating those around him as if they are the problem.

In leadership, there's often an elusive but undeniable sense we call gut instinct—those moments when your internal compass seems to pull you towards a decision without an obvious logical rationale. Honing this instinct can elevate your leadership to a new level, and the best way to sharpen it is through thoughtful reflection and tracking. That's where a *decision journal* comes into play. By keeping a record of these gut feelings, along with their outcomes, you'll be able to spot patterns, learn when your instincts are sharpest, and improve your overall decision-making process.

Decision Journaling

> *In my experience, the biggest challenge people face is learning to get out of their own way*[5]
> **Richard Bandler**

First things first, you'll need a system that works for you: a digital journal—something like *Evernote*, *OneNote*, or a simple document—or, if you are old school like me, a physical notebook. Your preference doesn't matter. What does matter is <u>self-discipline</u> and <u>consistency</u>. Every time you log a gut feeling, be sure to include these basics:

- *Date* of the decision
- *Description of the decision* you're grappling with and the feeling it stirred
- *Context* and environment (Were you rushed? Was the decision complex?)
- *Rationale-to-Instinct* (R/I) *Ratio* (How much of this decision was driven by logic versus instinct?)
- *Expected Outcome* versus *Actual Outcome*

This framework will guide you in building a clearer picture of how your instincts play out over time.

Start by becoming more mindful of those moments when your gut feeling kicks in. They can sneak up on you during a meeting, as you respond to emails, or when you're making a high-level strategic call. When you sense a strong gut reaction, jot it down. Here's how you can make that entry more meaningful:

1. **Be Specific About the Feeling**

Don't just record "I had a bad feeling." Be precise: Was it excitement or fear? Did it feel like a 'yes' or a 'no'? Was the decision attractive or repulsive? The more you label the feeling, the more you'll start to understand its origins.

- ***Pro tip***: *Notice where in your body the feeling appeared first. Was it in your chest? Did it move to your stomach? Perhaps it stayed in one spot or looped back around. Getting granular like this can help uncover patterns you might not notice otherwise.*

2. **Context is Crucial**

What was happening around you at the time? Were emotions running high? Did you have all the facts, or were you shooting from the hip due to time pressure? By capturing the context, you'll start to see whether certain environments amplify or mute your instincts.

3. **Track the Rationale-to-Instinct (R:I) Ratio**

Reflect on how much of the decision was based on cold, hard facts and how much relied on your gut. Use simple ratios like 50:50 or 80:20. Over time, you'll get a clearer picture of when your gut is most reliable and when it might need a logic check.

Monitor the Outcome

Decisions unfold at their own pace. Some outcomes are immediate, while others take weeks or months to come into focus. To make sure you don't forget, set reminders in your calendar or task management apps to review each decision at an appropriate interval.

When you come back to it, update your journal:

- Was the decision successful?
- Did your gut feeling guide you well, or did the outcome stray from your expectations?

- Were there any external factors or new information that changed the result?

This follow-up step is essential to learning from your instincts and improving your decision-making.

Review and Reflect on Patterns

Now that you've been logging your decisions, it's time to step back and review. Aim to do this once a month or once a quarter, depending on how frequently you've made entries. As you go through your journal, start identifying patterns:

1. **Look for Common Themes**

Are your gut instincts sharper in certain situations, like high-pressure environments or people-focused decisions? Or, conversely, are there times when they've led you astray, like when you didn't have enough data or felt rushed?

2. **Refine Your Self-Awareness**

Based on your reflections, fine-tune your approach. Are there moments when you need to trust your instincts more? Or situations where external pressures, biases, or emotions might cloud your judgment? This ongoing self-assessment will make you more conscious of when and how to rely on your gut feelings.

Consistency Imperative

The secret to success with this system is *consistency*. Keep up with your journaling, and over time, you'll collect enough data to see real patterns in your decision-making. But don't be too rigid either. The goal here is not to put your gut instinct on autopilot, but to blend it thoughtfully with rational analysis for more well-rounded decisions.

By consciously reflecting on your gut instincts, you can deepen your understanding of when to trust them and when to back them up with logic. The result? More informed, confident decisions—and leadership that feels both intuitive and grounded in reason.

This approach creates a reliable framework for personal growth and development, making you not just a leader who follows their gut, but one who hones it into a trusted tool for long-term success.

Balancing Instinct with Reason

In contrast with Mick, his brother, Ben, is known for his bold, innovative approach. Ben's leadership is characterised by quick intuitive decision-making, a willingness to take calculated risks, and an ability to inspire his team to push boundaries.

Ben's unconscious navigator seems to be calibrated differently. His neuroception is less sensitive to potential threats and more attuned to opportunities. This stems from a history of successful risk-taking.

While Ben's approach has led to breakthroughs and rapid growth, it also comes with its own set of challenges. He often overlooks genuine risks, pushes his team too hard in pursuit of his vision. His deep trust of his intuitions means that he will commit to large capital expenditures, without seeking Mick's agreement. To put it mildly, this 'seek forgiveness not permission' approach has become a source of explosive tension with Mick, who then obsesses about the downside.

Both Mick and Ben could benefit from a greater awareness of how their *unconscious navigator* is influencing their leadership style. For Mick, this has meant learning to question his instinctive caution, consciously looking for opportunities where his gut tells him to retreat. For Ben, it could involve developing practices to pause and reflect before acting on his intuitions, ensuring his risk-taking is truly calculated rather than impulsive.

Let's consider the practice of *Connect with Yourself*—that part of you that I've labelled *Unconscious Navigator*[6]. A rather simple yet profoundly effective method for those moments when life overwhelms you, when stress invades your body or your thoughts swirl restlessly. This technique offers not only rapid relief, often within a mere minute, but also the potential for deeper insight into how you might improve your current circumstances[7].

CONNECT with Yourself[8]

> "When you practice using your brain in this way, you will find yourself feeling really good a lot more often"
> **Richard Bandler**

First, acknowledge the stress you're experiencing. It's crucial to recognise when your body is holding onto tension or when your mind is entangled in an endless loop of racing thoughts. This act of recognition is the initial step towards regaining control—almost as if, by merely noticing it, you begin to dismantle its grip.

Next, shift your attention to one inch below your bellybutton. There's something curiously grounding about this. Think of a colour which, for you represents 'joy'. Any colour will do, so long as it means joy to you and a light with that right there. Place your hand gently over the light, just under your bellybutton. Let your focus settle on the sensation of your hand resting there.

Take three slow, deliberate breaths and breathe into your 'joy' light. Feel your tummy move gently in and out. It's not the breath itself that's the magic here—it's the concentration, the return of your awareness to the body's centre, to your core, that initiates a calming effect. With each breath, you'll likely feel a gentle release, a loosening of that earlier tension.

Then, recall a moment of joy. It could be anything—a memory of happiness, love, or deep contentment. Allow yourself to step back into that experience fully. What can you see, what can you hear, how does it feel? Engage with the memory as though it's unfolding again right now, in the present. Let the colours become brighter and more vivid, and the sounds be crisper and richer. And let the feeling be stronger and more intense. In doing this, you're not simply distracting yourself; you're actively shifting your emotional state, reorienting your mind and body towards positivity.

And here's where it becomes interesting: as you settle into that feeling of grounded safety, imagine that your *Unconscious Navigator* can speak. What might it tell you? What advice would it give you in this moment? This isn't about grand biblical revelations but rather subtle wisdom—often your body knows what you need before your mind has had a chance to catch up.

Finally, act on what you've learned. Whatever small or large step emerges from this quiet dialogue with yourself, follow through as soon as you can. It's the act of listening and then doing that transforms this simple practice into something truly powerful.

By engaging in this, you're not just calming yourself; you're developing a deeper relationship with your own inner signals—signals that, more often than not, offer a clearer sense of direction than the noise of everyday life.

SECTION ONE SUMMARY

*The answer, my friend,
is <u>not</u> blowing in the wind*
Keith McCullough

The *Instinctual Foundations* part of *Neuro-Resilience Skills* delves into the primal instincts that underpin leadership decisions and behaviours. By examining the neurological and physiological roots of gut instincts, this part empowers leaders to understand, refine, and leverage their natural responses to navigate the complexities of leadership effectively.

The journey begins in Chapter 1, *Instinctual Contact*, which explores the visceral, immediate reactions that arise from our ancient survival mechanisms. These instincts, honed through evolution, serve as our primal compass in uncertain or threatening situations. The chapter explains how our "second brain," the enteric nervous system, communicates with the central nervous system, influencing both our emotions and decisions. Leaders are introduced to the *Tension Releasor*, a technique for achieving metabolic congruence—aligning their internal state with the external environment to foster clarity and poise under pressure.

Chapter 2, *Instinctual Awareness*, introduces the Triune Brain Theory as a framework for understanding how instinct, emotion, and reason interplay in decision-making. The Reptilian Brain governs our survival instincts, the Mammalian Brain manages emotions and social bonds, and the Primate Brain enables logical reasoning and foresight. Leaders learn how to recognise when these brain layers align or conflict, particularly in high-stakes scenarios. Through the *Dual-Mind Reflection*, they are guided to pause, assess, and harmonise gut feelings with rational analysis, achieving more balanced and effective decisions.

In Chapter 3, *Instinctual Acuity*, the focus shifts to the unconscious processes that guide our behaviours and perceptions. The concept of neuroception—our nervous system's ability to detect safety or danger without conscious thought—takes centre stage, revealing how these subtle cues shape our responses. Leaders explore how unconscious vigilance can provide invaluable insights but also lead to overreactions if unchecked. The chapter introduces techniques like *The Worry Solver*, which transforms stress into actionable clarity, and *Connect with Yourself*, which helps leaders ground themselves in moments of overwhelm. By honing their "Unconscious Navigator," leaders can develop sharper instincts and greater self-awareness, enabling them to make more confident, congruent decisions.

Throughout this part, real-world examples and case stories illustrate how instincts play out in leadership contexts. From a CEO grappling with a major merger decision to contrasting leadership styles driven by risk-aversion or boldness, these narratives highlight the dual-edged nature of instincts. Leaders are encouraged to reflect on their own patterns and biases, using the tools provided to refine their instinctual responses.

SECTION ONE SUMMARY

The *Instinctual Foundations* part equips leaders with a deeper understanding of their primal instincts, helping them harness these ancient systems to thrive in modern leadership. By integrating instinct, emotion, and reason, leaders can foster resilience, clarity, and congruence in their decisions and actions.

Techniques Introduced:

- **Somatic Honing** – Develop grounded, intuitive decision-making.
- **Tension Releasor** – Achieve metabolic congruence and calm under pressure.
- **Dual-Mind Reflection** – Balance gut feelings with rational analysis.
- **The Worry Solver** – Transform worry into actionable clarity and control.
- **Decision Journaling** – Track and refine instinct-driven decisions.
- **Connect with Yourself** – Reduce stress and foster self-awareness.

These techniques form the foundation for leaders to develop greater neuro-resilience, integrating their instinctual and rational capacities for more effective and balanced leadership. By mastering these skills, leaders can navigate uncertainty with confidence and authenticity, leveraging the wisdom of their instincts as a powerful leadership tool.

Instinctual Awareness Exercises

Somatic Honing

1. Relax into a comfortable position in a quiet space where you won't be disturbed
2. Begin by taking a few slow, deep breaths
3. Inhale through your nose and exhale through your mouth
4. Focus on the rhythm of your breathing to settle your mind
5. Beginning at your toes, shift your attention slowly upwards through your body
6. As you do so, notice any sensations, such as tension, warmth, or discomfort
7. As you move up your legs, just sense without judgment or the need to react
8. Move your attention to your tummy and all the area below your diaphragm
9. Become aware of any sensations that you feel whether comfortable or stressful
10. Feel the effect your breath in your tummy and then feel it in your chest
11. Bring awareness to your shoulders, neck, and head
12. Observe any tension or relaxation in your muscles and your jawline
13. Once you've scanned your entire body, take five deep, cleansing breaths
14. Recall the sensations you noticed, especially in your tummy, chest, neck and head.

Tension Releasor

As this works best as an 'eyes closed' process, as it removes visual stimuli and allows you to focus on physical sensations. It's a straightforward technique but read the steps through a couple of times.

1. Inside of your mind, use a *calm gentle caring <u>inner</u> voice* to narrate the words below
2. Your words should feel like somewhere between a *command* and a *suggestion*; because it's a gentle *invitation* for your body, ever so softly, ever so gently, really relax
3. As you start engaging each body part, from the top of your head down to your feet, move your conscious awareness through to each body part.
4. If you find tension, move your awareness through it like a masseur would move their thumb gently through a knot
5. Take your time with each body part: be thorough before moving onto another.

Head

- My *scalp* can soften and relax now...
- My *eyes* can soften and relax now...
- My *mouth* can soften and relax now...
- My *tongue* can soften and relax now...
- My *jaw* can soften and relax now...

Neck, Shoulders & Arms

- My *neck* can soften and relax now...
- My *shoulders* can soften and relax now...
- My *arms* can soften and relax now...
- My *hands* can soften and relax now...

Back & Glutes

- My *upper back* can soften and relax now...
- My *lower back* can soften and relax now...
- My *glutes* can soften and relax now...

Legs & Feet

- My *thighs* can soften and relax now...
- My *calves* can soften and relax now...
- My *feet* can soften and relax now...

And now my **mind** can soften and relax still more and more...

Pause for a little while to notice the feelings and then, if you wish, repeat the exercise. Stay with this increasingly relaxed and calm feeling as long as you wish. You will be able to return to full waking alertness, refreshed and alert, as soon as you are ready.

Dual-Mind Reflection

Purpose:

The *Dual-Mind Reflection* trains leaders to take a brief pause before making major decisions. During this pause, they can reflect on both rational analysis and gut feelings. It helps leaders slow down and make more mindful choices, especially under pressure.

Steps:

1. When a major decision is required, mentally note that you are about to make a choice. This small step stops things just running automatically, creating the space for a more deliberate approach.
2. Before proceeding, take a slow, deep breath to signal a pause. This helps disengage any immediate emotional reactions and shifts your mind into a more reflective state.
3. Begin the 4-7-8 Breathing Technique
   - *Inhale* through your nose for a count of 4 seconds.
   - *Hold* your breath for 7 seconds.
   - *Exhale* slowly and completely through your mouth for 8 seconds. Repeat this cycle 3-4 times to calm your nervous system and clear your mind.
4. After calming your body with the 4-7-8 breathing, reflect on the rational aspects of the decision. What facts or data do you have? What are the logical pros and cons?
5. Now, shift attention to your gut feelings. How does this decision make you feel emotionally? Do you sense excitement, hesitation, or discomfort? Honour these gut reactions as valuable sources of insight.
6. Pay attention to any physical sensations or tension in your body during this pause. Areas like your gut or chest may provide clues about hidden stress or discomfort related to the decision.

7. Now that you've reviewed both your rational analysis and gut feelings, balance the two perspectives. Are they aligned? Do they offer contrasting views?
8. After reflecting on both the logical and intuitive aspects, proceed with your decision. Trust that by pausing, you've gained a fuller, more holistic understanding of the situation.

The Worry Solver

1. Begin by focusing on something that has been causing you concern.
2. Ask yourself:
   - "What is the underlying purpose of this worry?
   - How is it trying to help me?
   - What does it provide or protect me from?

Be specific because the answer is often something related to safety or protection

3. Once you've identified the reason that resonates with you, challenge your Primate Brain, the rational mind, to find at least three different way to achieve the same positive outcome without the burden of stress or discomfort that comes with worrying.
4. Make sure you feel completely at ease with these new options. If you sense any reluctance, take a moment to ask your mind to resolve any inner disagreements. You will know you're ready when you feel peaceful and confident about moving forward with these alternatives.

Finally, visualise yourself applying these new approaches in the future at least five times or until it feels natural, as though it's the way you've always handled things.

Decision Journaling

1. **Choose Your Journal** – Use a digital tool or notebook; consistency matters more than format.
2. **Log Your Decisions** – Track key moments in meetings, emails, and strategic choices:

   - **Date** – When did the gut feeling occur?
   - **Decision & Feelings** – Briefly describe both.
   - **Context** – Was it rushed, complex, or personal?
   - **R/I Ratio** – Estimate the mix of reason vs. instinct.
   - **Expected vs. Actual** – Measure decision accuracy.

3. **Be Specific About the Feeling**
   - Was it excitement, fear, certainty, or doubt?
   - Where did you feel it first (chest, stomach, etc.)?
4. **Capture the Context**
   - What was happening? Were emotions high? Did you have all the facts?
   - Identify environments that amplify or mute your instincts.
5. **Track the R/I Ratio**
   - Estimate the balance (e.g., 50:50, 80:20).
   - Over time, notice when your gut is reliable vs. when logic is needed.
6. **Monitor the Outcome**
   - Schedule periodic reviews (monthly/quarterly).
   - Reflect: Was your gut right? Did new information change the result?
7. **Review and Identify Patterns**
   - When are your instincts sharpest? When have they misled you?
   - Recognise when to lean on instinct vs. reason.
8. **Stay Consistent**

- Keep tracking to refine your instinct-reason balance.
- Recognise that different decisions (e.g., lunch vs. house purchase) require different ratios.

9. **Learn and Grow**
    - Develop confidence in balancing intuition with logic.
    - Become a leader who makes informed, intuitive decisions.

Connect with Yourself

1. Recognise the tension in your body or the racing thoughts in your mind.

   - Notice how you feel. This recognition alone starts to lessen the stress, as you begin to take back control.

2. As you shift your attention to a point about one inch below your bellybutton:

   - Think of the kind of intense joy that child have
   - Visualise a colour that represents that level of joy
   - Let that colour form into a light on that spot below your bellybutton
   - Place your hand gently over this spot and focus on the sensation of your hand resting there.

3. Take three slow, deep breaths, focusing on your 'joy' light.

   - As you breathe, feel your tummy gently rise and fall.
   - With each breath, notice how the tension begins to loosen, as you centre your awareness on your core.

4. Think of a joyful memory—a time when you felt happy, loved, or content:

   - Relive that moment in your mind. What do you see, hear, and feel?
   - Engage with this memory fully, as though it is happening now
   - Allow yourself to immerse in the positive emotions it brings

5. Settle into the feeling of calm and safety

- Imagine that your *Unconscious Navigator* can speak to you.
- Use your intuition sense any insights or subtle wisdom.
- Ask yourself:
    - *"What might it say? What advice does it offer?"*

6. Act on Your Insight

- This wisdom comes from a part of your being. Whether it's a small adjustment or a larger change, follow through as soon as possible.
- Acting on this inner wisdom turns this practice into a powerful tool for personal growth and direction.

PART TWO
PERSONAL RESILIENCE SKILLS

INTRODUCTION

*If you know the enemy and know yourself,
you need not fear the result of a hundred battles*
Sun Tzu

In a world increasingly defined by complexity, uncertainty, and relentless demands, resilience is no longer a luxury but a necessity. For leaders, the stakes are even higher. Whether navigating a high-stakes negotiation, leading a team through layoffs, or managing personal crises while maintaining professional poise, leaders face challenges that test not just their intellect but their emotional and physiological thresholds. The three chapters in this part—*Core Skills*, *Intermediate Skills*, and *Advanced Skills*—offer a roadmap for developing neuro-resilience, an essential skillset for thriving under pressure and emerging stronger from adversity.

At the heart of this journey lies an understanding of our most primal instincts. Conceive of the moment a gazelle, grazing peacefully, senses a predator nearby. Without conscious thought, its body shifts into *mobilisation* or *immobilisation*, survival strategies deeply ingrained in its neurobiology. While humans are far removed from the savanna, these instinctive responses persist, influencing how we react to stressors in the workplace today. Recognising and mastering these primal forces is the foundation of personal resilience.

Understanding the Core

In *Chapter 4: Core Skills*, we begin with the basics—an exploration of how our body's primal instincts manifest in everyday life. Drawing on principles from neuro-linguistic programming (NLP) and the wisdom of ancient maxims like "know thyself," this chapter invites readers to map their internal responses. By uncovering patterns in their sensory modalities—visual, auditory, and kinaesthetic—leaders gain a clearer picture of how their body reacts to both positive and negative stimuli. This deep self-awareness lays the groundwork for a nuanced understanding of stress responses and their influence on decision-making, social engagement, and professional performance.

Through practical exercises such as *Instinct Mapping* and *Finding Home*, readers learn to bridge the gap between their conscious and unconscious responses. These tools empower leaders to move from reaction to intention, transforming instinctive impulses into purposeful actions.

Steadying the Ship

Building on this foundation, *Chapter 5: Intermediate Skills* delves into strategies for maintaining balance in turbulent times. Neuro-resilience, as illustrated through the metaphor of a seasoned ship captain steering through a storm, is about navigating crises with clarity and composure. Leaders are introduced to techniques like *Stepping Out of Fear* and *Taming Vicious Memories*, which help recalibrate physiological responses to perceived threats. These methods are not just about managing stress but about reprogramming the mind to perceive challenges with curiosity rather than fear[1].

Through relatable case stories, such as Rebecca's journey from reactive to responsive leadership, readers see how these tools can be applied to real-world situations. By learning to distinguish between instinctual reactions and thoughtful responses, leaders gain the ability to make better decisions, inspire confidence, and create an environment of psychological safety.

Mastering the Inner Game

Finally, *Chapter 6: Advanced Skills* challenges readers to elevate their resilience to a level of instinctual intelligence. This is where the journey moves beyond self-awareness and self-regulation into the realm of mastery. Advanced techniques like *Turning Anxiety Around* and *Wrapped in Serenity* help leaders transform negative emotional states into positive, productive ones. By actively engaging with and manipulating their internal experiences, leaders learn to harness the power of their instincts rather than being dominated by them.

This chapter introduces a four-tier model of instinctual development: *Instinct Ignorance, Instinct Awareness, Instinct Acuity,* and *Instinct Intelligence.* The progression through these stages reflects a leader's journey from being at the mercy of their physiological responses to leveraging them as tools for growth, creativity, and leadership excellence.

Why Resilience Matters

The skills presented in this part are not theoretical abstractions; they are practical, actionable techniques honed through years of research and application. They are designed to help leaders confront the realities of today's business—a landscape fraught with unpredictability and high stakes. More importantly, they offer a path to personal growth that extends beyond the workplace. By mastering these inner games, leaders can bring their best selves to every arena of life, fostering trust, collaboration, and resilience within their teams and organisations.

This part is not just about survival; it's about thriving. It's about understanding that our instincts, while rooted in evolutionary biology, can be guided, shaped, and even rewired to serve us in today's complex world[2]. With these skills, leaders will be better equipped to face challenges head-on, emerging not just unscathed but stronger, wiser, and more capable than before. Welcome to the journey of mastering your personal resilience skills. Let's begin.

FOUR
CORE SKILLS

The body knows things about which the mind is ignorant[1]
Jacques Lecoq

RETHINK about that gazelle grazing peacefully on the African savanna. Suddenly, it catches the scent of a predator on the wind. In an instant, its entire physiology shifts. Muscles tense, heart rate accelerates, pupils dilate. The gazelle is poised on a knife-edge, ready to explode into action at the slightest provocation. This is mobilisation in its purest form.

Now, imagine that same gazelle, but this time it's too late. The predator is upon it. In a flash, the gazelle's body goes limp, its heart rate plummets, and it enters a state of profound stillness. This is immobilisation—nature's last-ditch survival strategy.

In neither case does the gazelle cognitively chose the mobilised and immobilised responses. They are entirely chosen by the gazelle's *body* bypassing its conscious awareness. These *unconscious choices* are not merely the province of wild animals. They are deeply embedded in our own neurobiology too, as humans have a shared mammalian ancestry with the gazelle. As it was put more beautifully in *The Descent of Man*[2]:

> *Man still bears in his bodily frame the indelible stamp of his lowly origin*
> **Charles Darwin**

They continue to determine our responses to perceived threats in the digital age society, *including the workplace and including top executives*. You, that is, the conscious 'you', does not choose your response. Your body does that itself. The conscious 'you' come up with justifying reason 'why' your body responded that way, afterwards.

This is important because it doesn't feel like that, but that's how mammalian bodies function. The separation is not between the 'mind' and the 'body', it's a sequencing of the 'unconscious' and 'unconscious' responses in both the brain and the rest of the body. Let's consider how these primordial responses might manifest in our contemporary professional lives:

Picture Samantha, an experienced and capable Senior Business Development Manager. She is getting ready for a high-stakes meeting. As she prepares to present a crucial proposal, she feels her heart racing, her palms growing sweaty. Her senses sharpen, her mind becomes hyper-focused. This is mobilisation at work—her body preparing her to face a challenge, not so different from our gazelle preparing to flee from a predator.

In many ways, this mobilised response can be adaptive *in the workplace. It can sharpen our focus, enhance our performance, and push us to rise to challenges. It's what allows us to meet tight deadlines, think on our feet during difficult negotiations, or rally a team in times of crisis.*

In NLP, the qualities of our senses become hidden doorways to our primal instincts. We all experience those powerful instinctual responses that pull us towards something we desire or push us away from something repelling.

Through the following fascinating technique, you will learn how your individual sense modalities of seeing (**V**isual), hearing (**A**uditory) and feeling (**K**inaesthetic) are represented differently by our nervous system. The different qualities and characteristics of these VAK modalities are called _sub_modalities, which is where your unique patterns are hidden.

As inscribed in the *Temple of Apollo* at Delphi is a famous maxim, 'know thyself'. It is important to note that it is *your particular* nervous system that you are about to explore. It will be thinking about a particular thing that *you* have chosen to think about. As such, this is a study of *your* subjective experience, not someone else's and certainly not everyone else's. This is a good thing because you'll uncover the sensory patterns that underpin *your* primal responses, specifically.

Since you'll need a reasonable degree of concentration, settle in somewhere peaceful, free from distractions, so you can focus entirely on your internal world. This exercise is most effective when you can immerse yourself without interruption. Be clear of the mission: you're here to uncover how *your* primal instincts manifest in your VAK submodalities.

Instinct Mapping[3]

> *In order to change beliefs, we first need to learn a way of finding out the qualities of beliefs*
> **Richard Bandler**

First think of one "move towards" instinctual response that you enjoy, such as lust or greed or desire; as well as one "move away from" response that you strongly dislike, like disgust, fear, or sadness. Write them down ahead of time.

Close your eyes and summon a vivid memory of a time when you felt a deep sense of lust or greed. These are base primal mammalian instincts that might be inappropriate conversations in the staff canteen. However, they are a part of you and, for good or ill, these primal drives drive your decisions. So, to uncover their patterns, the intensity of these primal feelings needs to be life and death intensity; not like you're going window shopping.

So, if it's lust, think of a time you were emersed in a lustful moment, completely locked into to that primal desire. If it's greed, remember an experience that you were intensely feeling,

"I want that! I'm taking it! That's mine!".

Whatever the instinct that you have picked, you want to be as aroused and focused as a starving man smelling meat on the barbeque. That's the level of primal instinctive intensity you require.

So, re-live the moment clearly by: 1) seeing what you saw through your eyes at the time; 2) hear what you heard through your ears and 3) feeling the strong primal urge building in your body. Now, make the pictures brighter and bolder, make the sounds richer and crisper and allow the sensations to intensify.

Now, holding everything at max intensity, make a note of the VAK qualities:

- **Visual**: Is the image bright or dim? Is it a movie or a still? Is it in colour or black and white? Is it sharp and in focused or is it a grainy or blurry? Are the colours vivid or dull? Is the image close to you, or does it seem distant? Is it 3D or flat?

- **Auditory**: Are there sounds in this memory? Are they loud or soft? Is the sound clear or muffled? Do the sounds seem to come from inside your head going out, or do they seem external coming towards you? Are there voices present? If so, what's the tone—seductive, calm, or something else?

- **Kinaesthetic**: Where do you feel the sensation in your body? How does it move through your body? Is it moving down/ up or left/ right? Do they feel warm or cool, sharp or soft? Is it a heavy or light feeling? Are you breathing high and fast at the top of your chest or low and slow in your abdomen?

Use the '*Submodality Comparison*' sheets in 'Appendix' and check off/ tick everything you've noticed about the characteristics and the qualities of the pictures, sounds, and feelings of this positive, instinctual response. If you detect tastes or smells check off/ tick them too. Remember: this is all about how *your* body and brain codes your thoughts, feelings and memories.

Then re-run the exercise for the negative instinct. I know that it is not fun doing strong negative feelings, so I would encourage you to do them really well, otherwise you'll need to repeat it (which really sucks!). So, again, if it's fear, think of a time where you were really scared. If it's disgust, make it an experience you had that was absolutely gross. Whatever the negative instinct that you have picked, you want to be as aroused and focused as a terrified gazelle running for its life. That's the level of primal instinctive intensity you require.

These are your experiences, so you might as well make the most of them and, hopefully, for the last time.

With both sets of notes before you, look for the *difference* not the similarities. For example, if both pictures are grainy doesn't matter. If the sounds are muffled in both, or you are panting in both, these qualities do not matter. However, if one memory had a yellow hue and the other was more of a blue hue; if one picture had a border around it and the other didn't, that's important.

If one had sound coming in from the left and the other from the right; or one was loud and the other was silent, that's important. If the feelings with one seemed to circle in the tummy and the other was like it was shooting up your legs, that's important. If you could taste or smell something in one and something different (or nothing at all) in the other, that's what is important.

When Your Body's Lost Its Way

By mapping and comparing the submodalities of different states, you've laid the groundwork to understand how you respond to life's most instinctual moments. This is your opportunity to calibrate to your unique internal patterns. By doing so, your *instinct acuity* is a magnitude higher than most leaders. You have begun to know yourself in a more useful and unique way. But as Sophocles put in *Oedipus Rex*:

"Alas, how terrible is wisdom when it brings no profit to the man that's wise!

Because we can all get knocked off kilter, from time to time, and lose our way. Perhaps something has happened in our personal relationship, or some other disappointment has befallen us. Either way, as professionals we need to be able to get back to how we normally are. Or perhaps it's a problem in business and we don't want to contaminate our home life, with cranky intolerance, domestic tension and interrupted sleep. How can we get our old selves back?

This is a great point in the book to learn a method that, with practice, will allow you to take control of your stress for the rest of your life. I call it *Finding Home*.

This process is not about eliminating stress entirely—after all, some stress is part of being alive—but rather about training your mind to handle it with grace, to meet life's challenges from a place of calm, rather than tension.

FINDING HOME

We begin by bringing clarity to the present sources of your stress. Take a few moments now to reflect and identify the five most significant sources of stress that are weighing on you. Write them down, if you can. There's something powerful in the act of naming them—by writing them out, you begin to gain control over them, shifting them from vague feelings to clear, tangible things you can work with.

Once you've compiled your list, we will go through each stressor, one by one. This will be an exercise in reducing their power over you. By doing so, you're also training your unconscious mind to maintain a lower overall stress level, a more natural state of ease. Please read and understand (even write down) the instructions before you begin. As an aid, all exercises are in short form at the end of the part.

Let's start with one stressor from your list. I want to create a calm anchor. Remembering the feeling of calm in the 'Connect with Yourself'. Go can just re-live the exercise in your mind: see what you saw, hear what you heard and feeling that lovely feeling of calm. Make the colours, sounds and sensations beautiful to you. Then press your thumb and middle finger together. And, as you press them together, take a deep, steady breath and find that the corners of your mouth are turning up into a little smile.

Think of the face of your favourite comedian. Notice that their face alone can bring you a smile. Because, neurologically, when things that are fired together are wired together. Their face, perhaps their voice. But when you think of it, it triggers a smile. As that feeling of calm joy peak, again press your thumb and finger to together. This is called *anchoring* because it ties the stimulus to the response. When you *fire the anchor*, the body will recall the feeling.

Now, bring to mind the stressful situation you've chosen, but hold it lightly. Picture yourself facing it, but with an unusual twist: imagine that you're looking at it with complete ease.

As this scene unfolds in your mind, let that sense of calm, initiated by your anchor, spread through your body. Now, visualise yourself moving through the situation smoothly. Picture what you'll see. Hear the sounds around you, the voices, the background hum of life. Feel how peaceful you are. Every movement, every decision, every interaction feels effortless. You are in control, not through force, but through calm presence.

Fire the anchor (press the thumb and finger together) and bring back calm and confident feeling. Now, bring the stressful situation to mind again, but this time, add a layer of complexity. Imagine that a few challenges arise—maybe the situation doesn't go perfectly, maybe things don't unfold exactly as planned. But here's the key: watch as you handle those challenges with the same calm ease. Again, see what you'll see, hear what you'll hear, and most importantly, feel the sense of calm as you navigate these obstacles effortlessly.

Pause for a moment. Reflect on how you feel now, in relation to that stressor. Does it feel different than it did a few minutes ago? Can you sense a shift in how your body is responding to it? If not, don't worry —sometimes these things take time, and *the beauty of this practice is in its repetition.* Simply repeat the process as needed, allowing your mind and body to adjust to this new way of being.

Now, repeat this exercise for the remaining stressors on your list. Take your time with each one, using your calm anchor to guide you back to that place of ease and control. With each round, you're not only reducing the power of these individual stressors, but you're also teaching your mind a new pattern. You're training it to generalise this calmness across your entire life, a calm that extends beyond these specific situations.

And here's the real power: as you continue to practice, you'll find that your unconscious mind starts adopting this lower stress level as its default state. Stressors will still come and go, but your baseline will be different—a foundation of calm resilience, ready to handle whatever life throws your way.

As we conclude this exploration of our body's responses in the workplace, let's return to our friend Samantha. Armed with this understanding of her own nervous system, she might approach that high-stakes presentation differently. She might recognise her racing heart not as anxiety to be suppressed, but as her body's way of rising to a challenge. She might use grounding techniques to modulate her activation, finding the sweet spot where she's energised but not overwhelmed.

And if she finds herself freezing in the face of harsh criticism? She might recognise this as an adaptive response to perceived threat and take steps to re-engage her social nervous system—perhaps by connecting with a supportive colleague or using breath work to shift her physiological state.

In our next chapter, we'll explore practical strategies for fostering this kind of nervous system literacy in the workplace, examining how organisations can create environments that support resilience, recovery, and the cultivation of our innate capacity for social engagement.

FIVE
INTERMEDIATE SKILLS

Rock bottom became the solid foundation on which I rebuilt my life
J.K. Rowling

SALTY SEAMEN STEERING through a perfect storm. The lashing rain and howling wind, the impenetrable blanket of darkness, and the relentless crashing of waves could easily overwhelm even the bravest souls. Yet, the captain stands steady at the helm, his demeanour a reflection of his calm poise and focus—a beacon of hope for the anxious crew. This is the essence of neuro-resilience in leadership—the ability to maintain equilibrium and effectiveness, even in the face of overwhelming challenges.

As we venture deeper into the complex terrain of instinct and leadership, we arrive at a critical juncture: how can leaders develop the personal capacity to navigate the turbulent waters of instinctual and emotional responses? And let's be honest, we've all been there, haven't we? Faced with unexpected challenges that trigger something primal within us? The answer lies in cultivating neuro-resilience—a set of skills that enables leaders not only to weather the storm themselves but also to guide their teams through it.

The Case for *Neuro-Resilience*

Present day leaders face unprecedented levels of complexity, uncertainty and stress, from rapidly changing demographics, to fluctuating regulations and exponential advances in technology. Have you ever noticed that no matter how much strategic planning you do, some situations hit you in ways you didn't expect? That's because many challenges trigger our most primitive instinctual responses, bypassing rational thought processes and leading to reactive, suboptimal decisions.

Take Gary, the factory general manager. His finance manager, Rebecca, is well-versed in strategic planning, financial analysis, and team management. But when faced with a crisis that triggered her fight-or-flight response, all that knowledge went out the window, as her reptilian brain took over. Sound familiar? After Rebecca's 'blank mind' moment, Gary had her trained in neuro-resilience skills.

Months later, Gary tells her to prepare the planning for a series of layoffs. This announcement jolts her and her body responds in exactly the same way. This time, however, Rebecca understands that her body is having a reflex-like instinctual response called 'fight-or-flight'.

She understands that her body has chosen to go through a series of physiological *patterns of protection*: her brain's alarm system, the amygdala, has kicked into gear; stress hormones, like cortisol and adrenaline, are flooding her body; her heart rate and blood pressure are spiking; and blood flow is being redirected from her primate brain to the limbs, priming her for battle or to run.

Recognising this change of state, Rebecca takes a moment to begin to autoregulate, in order to access the higher cognitive functions in her primate brain. She uses the *Stepping Out of Fear* technique which is designed to help step back from stressful thoughts, creating both distance and clarity.

STEPPING *Out of Fear*

This method is particularly effective when you find yourself overwhelmed by emotions tied to a specific situation. Remember, Rebecca's mobilised response is not because there is actual danger in front of her. Rather, her brain has conjured pictures and sounds that are believable enough to her body, which then shifts into 'fight-or-flight. As imaginary problems require imaginary solutions, Rebecca understands that she must change the way she is imagining the situation to become calmer and more objective. Take a moment to read the instructions fully.

Start by bringing the source of your stress to mind. It could be a recent event or something from the past that still lingers. Perhaps it's a future worry that's playing on your mind. Whatever it is, take a moment to picture it.

This image might come to you as a collection of still frames—faces, locations, or specific moments. Or it could play like a short video, a scene unfolding in your mind. However, it appears to you is perfectly fine; the important thing is to bring it into focus in a way that feels natural.

Now, imagine stepping out of the scene entirely. Visualise yourself as if you were watching a film, but instead of being inside the action, you're floating gently away from it. Feel yourself moving back from your body, so you can now see the back of your head, as though you're observing yourself from a distance. Sometimes people find it easier visualising this by drifting out from the side and seeing themselves in profile. Whichever way works easiest, you will be able to see yourself in the movie. At the same time, your awareness is outside of the movie, watching it play out.

Keep moving away, until the scene is about three metres away from you. You're now viewing it from a safe distance, as though it's happening to someone else. In a similar way watching people on a rollercoaster from the ground is different from the firsthand experience of being in the rollercoaster. From this vantage point of three metres away, the situation feels less immediate, less overwhelming, allowing you to see it with a bit more objectivity.

Next, remove all the colour from the scene. Picture it as if it were an old black-and-white film. The vibrancy is gone, and with it, the emotional charge begins to dull even more. The movie is still playing, but it's stripped of the vividness that makes it feel so present.

Now, shrink the image down to a tenth of the original size. Picture the scene becoming smaller, more manageable. As it reduces in size, notice how your feelings towards it begin to shift. It's no longer looming over you—it is now something contained, something you can observe without feeling so affected.

Finally, make the image transparent. Let it fade, becoming lighter and more translucent, until it's barely there. You can still see it, but it no longer holds the same power. The scene, once so vivid and pressing, has now faded to a shadow of its former self[1].

With the emotional intensity reduced, you're in a better position to think clearly. Ask yourself: Are there any decisions you need to make about this situation? If so, make them now, from this calmer, more detached viewpoint. This distance allows you to see the problem without being entangled in its emotional web.

When you're ready, you can return to the present moment. The stressful image, now reduced, no longer holds the same weight. This practice, done regularly, can help you gain perspective on challenges that feel overwhelming, giving you space to respond thoughtfully rather than react emotionally.

In time, you'll find that this process becomes a natural response to stress, a way of reframing difficult situations and regaining your emotional balance.

PREVIOUS BAD EXPERIENCES

Rather than being triggered by imagining a danger that is not actually there, a fight-or-flight response is often triggered by memories of something that really happened. Because of their nature, these memories usually involve moments of adrenaline and noradrenaline associated with a mobilised response. Just as adrenaline in the body gives us the energy to fight or escape, noradrenaline is the equivalent for the brain, where it seems to make things slow down, visuals become more vivid, and our hearing is more acute. Our survival wisdom has put our body on instant high alert.

In a world of sabertoothed tigers, it is easy to understand how the ability to be stronger, faster, with sharper senses is an advantage to survival. However, after the event, these vivid pictures, crisp sounds and negative physical arousal can come back as very disturbing memories. This is especially so as they stand out starkly from other everyday memories like having a wonderful day at the beach or lovely meal with the family.

TAMING *Vicious Memories*[2]

Let's explore a powerful technique for transforming the emotional weight of a difficult memory. This exercise invites you to reframe the experience in a way that detaches it from the negative emotions that have been bound to it. Think of it as a kind of mental editing, where you become both the director and the viewer of your own film. All the exercises are listed in the end of the part in simple step 1, 2, 3 form. Before you do the exercises, read them through thorough here, so that you clear what to do.

To begin, see yourself sitting comfortably in a cozy cinema. The kind of seat that's so perfectly designed for relaxation, you feel at ease the moment you settle in. The lights are dim, the room is quiet, and everything is set for you to watch a film—not just any film, but one that you're going to re-edit for your own benefit.

Now, imagine that you can float out of your body, gently rising up towards the projection booth above. From this new vantage point behind the protective glass, you can see yourself seated below, completely relaxed, ready to watch the screen. You're still present, but in a way that feels distant from the scene unfolding before you.

On the screen, you're about to watch a troubling memory. But before it starts, identify two key moments: the first is just before the event took place—what you might call the ***before*** moment—and the second is just after you successfully navigated through the experience, the ***after*** moment. These two moments serve as the boundaries of the memory you're about to reframe.

Project a still image of the ***before*** moment onto the screen. From your safe spot in the projection booth, observe yourself seated in the cinema below, watching this image on the screen. This creates a layered distance between you and the memory—a gentle buffer of safety.

Now, let the film play. Watch the memory unfold from the ***before*** moment, moving all the way through to the ***after*** moment, where you've come out the other side. Once you reach the end of the event, freeze the frame on the screen at the ***after*** point, that moment where the difficult experience has passed, and you are safe.

Here's where the rewiring begins. In your mind, play the film in reverse, as quickly as possible. Watch everything rewind—the visuals, the sounds, even the sensations—all racing backwards to the ***before*** moment. Imagine the entire experience unravelling, like watching a tape reel spinning rapidly in reverse.

Repeat this process five times fast. Watch the memory play out, then swiftly rewind it back to the beginning. With each repetition, you will find that the emotional intensity lessens, you can recall the memory, but the intensity of feelings that you have are diminished. It's as if the memory has lost its sting, leaving you with a clearer, calmer perspective.

FAST & Easy Refresh

To further reinforce this process, consider engaging in regular relaxation practices, such as listening to a hypnotic trance, which can help dissolve any lingering discomfort.

SCAN THIS QR Code here for a lovely trance that lasts under ten minutes. It's a fast and easy way to move from the idea of altering your state to just doing it. I was asked to do a 'trance under 10' for someone in Orlando, Florida. This is a recording of that moment: cleaned up, enhanced and published.

Neuro-Spa

It can be done 'eyes open' or 'eyes closed' - it's under ten minutes long. Take the time and try both. Do then do it both ways a second time. Coming in and out of an altered state, trains your neurology to do it deliberately.

Through repetition, you're not just increasing your skill—you're training your mind to think in a different way, your body to feel a different way, which will lead you to choose do things differently. This is *personal freedom*.

Slowly *Then Suddenly*

We've discussed how getting sudden bad news or a sudden recollection of a bad experience can trigger a mobilised response, which downgrades our cognitive function. Another way leaders have learned to downgrade their cognition is by generating a gloomy view about themselves and their future.

It's not uncommon for even the best of leaders to hit a run of adverse results, none of which are directly related to their individual or even their team's performance. After all, in business, the 'Business Cycle' cycles through boom and bust. It is intellectually honest and will keep you grounded were you to admit it when your results are looking great without really deserving it. After all, sometime dumb luck can be lucky. On the other hand, congratulating yourself for good dumb luck is not only dishonest, but also deluded.

Dumb luck also has a double-edged sword because, at other times, dumb luck can be *unlucky*. Similarly, castigating yourself for bad dumb luck is not only dishonest, but also unnecessarily demoralising. Worse still, with a string of bad luck, you can begin to list into an emotional downward spiral, dragging your team along with you.

Once more, that spiral is a result of one's imagination, because you've built a belief from the conviction you have that the past predicts the future, the current trajectory will persist, and that cycles don't cycle. The brain then projects a visual hallucination of horrible things with a hideous internal dialogue pouring gasoline on the flames.

Again, this jolts your body into metabolic and behavioural *patterns of protection*. And, as long as the gloomy hallucinations continue, the protective patterns will continue; eventually becoming toxic. What is needed is a way of letting your emotional balance to naturally reset, creating the space for calm and clarity to emerge, once again.

. . .

Silencing the Storm[3]

Bring to your mind a situation that has been causing you stress or worry. It could be something recent or a long-standing issue that seems to resurface time and again. Take a moment to let this situation come into focus.

Now, pause and reflect on the narrative you've been telling yourself about this situation. Often, these stories sound something like:

- "There's nothing I can do, it's all going sideways again."
- "This is just the way things are in my department. There's just no way out."
- "I don't think I can handle this anymore. I'm beaten."
- "Why can't we ever get a break?"

It doesn't matter if the story is perfectly clear in your mind or if it's vague and unformed—simply allow yourself to connect with whatever *inner dialogue* feels familiar. If necessary, feel free to create an example that fits the gist of how you are feeling.

Now, turn your attention to that voice, the one repeating the gloomy narrative. Where does it seem to come from? Does it come in from the front, the back, the left- or right-hand side of your head? Or does it come from the inside out? If so, in which direction is it coming out? Just notice from where this internal dialogue seems to arise and go to.

Next, visualise those words, in their written form, leaving your mind. See them drifting outward, like subtitles in a film. Now, hear the same voice three metres away from you. As you hear the voice over there, still gibbering and whining away about the same old nonsense as it did inside your head. However, notice how your feelings have changed.

What happens when that story is no longer sitting inside your head but out there? This shift in perspective—moving the voice outside yourself—creates a kind of emotional shift. It helps your mind reframe the story, creating distance between you and the old narrative. With that narrative no longer looming inside you, you'll find there's room for something new now—something closer, better and more empowering.

At your own pace, begin to lower the volume of that distant voice. Let it grow quieter, softer, until it's barely audible, a whisper on the edge of your awareness. And as the volume fades, notice how it feels to no longer be tethered to that old story. And, in this newly cleared space, recognise that you have the freedom to create a new narrative.

By engaging in this practice, you are not just quieting the noise of self-doubt and worry—you are actively regulating your emotions, repairing your own safety. Preparing the groundwork for a better that moves you forward. And the more you do this, the more practice you put in, the more natural it will become, allowing you to regain your sense of safety.

By learning to *rewire* how the brain has encoded a horrible event, both real from the past and think about the present or the future, you open the door to a mind that is not only capable of healing but also of growing stronger through each of challenges. That is part of what I call the *Inner Game* of neuro-resilience skills.

SIX
ADVANCED SKILLS

So throw away your baggage and go forward
Aldous Huxley

THERE ARE LEVELS TO NLP. As such, we shall continue practical applications to build the skills and learning that leaders need to grow:

1. *Instinctual Ignorance* – where their metabolism and behaviours shift in a Pavlovian manner, which they do not understand but then justify to themselves after the event.
2. *Instinctual Awareness* – where they become conscious of how their instincts manifest in the feelings and sensation in the different part and all over their whole body.
3. *Instinctual Acuity* – where they become nuanced about their own neurological impulse that move us towards and away from things; how they manifest in their subjective experience, their VAK submodalities; how patterns of

protection present themselves; and how they affect their decisions.

4. *Instinctual Intelligence* – where they learn to trust their instincts when appropriate; as well as to engage with them to think differently, feel differently and act differently. They know umpteen ways to dial their negative feelings down, when they are being counterproductive. They know how to return to a state of safety, from the skin in, to make social engagement, problem-solving and decision-making fully available to us.

In the strategies in the last chapter, we learned highly effective with imaginary visual and auditory solutions to fight-flight responses, which were created by visual and auditory memories and hallucinations. These techniques are from NLP, specifically as they are taught by Dr. Richard Bandler, which is about finding what people actually do to get over their problems and systematising them, so that we can do it ourselves.

The system being, changing how we think (visually and auditorily) changes how we feel (instinctively and emotionally) changes how we act (socially and cognitively). As with almost all activities, people get better, faster and more precise the more often they do the activity. Practice makes perfect and 'perfect' is just a lot of little things done well.

This next technique, whilst using the same NLP technology, is a technique from an approach called *Neuro-Hypnotic Repatterning* (NHR), invented by Richard Bandler and is one of the most impactful and useful techniques. In this book, we shall use it, once more, to repair safety, in this case, your own.

Turning **Anxiety Around**[1]

> *"By reversing the spin of a negative emotion, you can transform it into a positive one"*
> **Richard Bandler**

Let's explore an approach to anxiety that takes us beyond merely acknowledging it and into the realm of actively engaging with how it feels in the body. Again, anxiety is an unpleasant feeling, so when you are practicing this technique, go all in so that you can learn the technique quickly and well.

Start by bringing to your mind something that makes you anxious or fearful. I can tell you, as a husband, father, brother and son, there are a number of things that could get me into a cold sweat in a heartbeat. So, if there is nothing making you anxious at present, make one up. As you focus on this, notice where the sensation of anxiety settles in your body. If you pay close attention, you'll find that it doesn't just sit still. In fact, anxiety often has a kind of spin to it, a movement that you can feel if you concentrate closely enough. This movement can take several forms.

For some, the anxiety might spin along the midline of the body, perhaps moving upward from the base of the torso, curving back down, and then repeating this upward and downward cycle. For others, it might move in the opposite direction, spinning downward, curving up, and then looping again. There's another possibility, where anxiety crosses from one side of the body to the other. It might rise up one side, cross over the midline at the top, descend the other side, and then come back up again. Or perhaps the motion starts lower, moving down one side, crossing at the bottom, and then rising again. Some people feel it more like a flat disc, spinning horizontally across the body, moving either left to right or right to left[2].

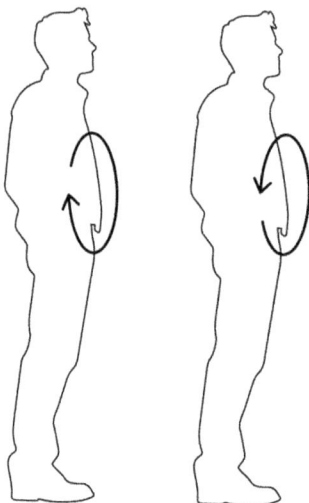

Spinning feeling coming up/ down the midline

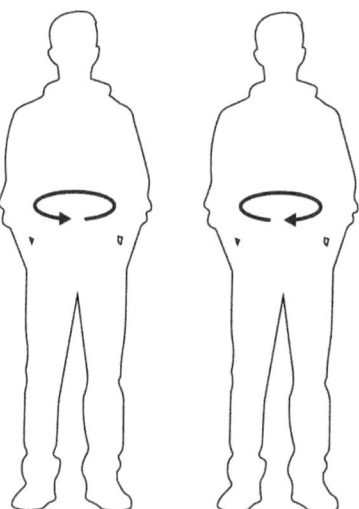

Spinning feeling like a flat disc, on/ crossing the midline

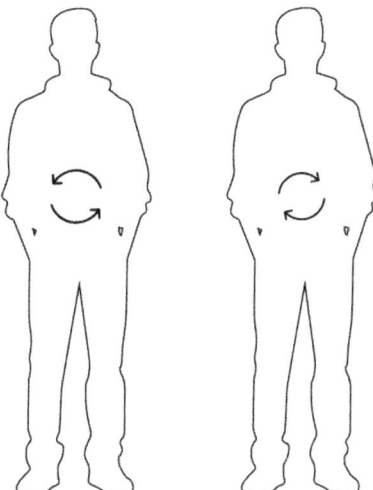

Spinning across the abdominal crossing the midline

Whichever way it moves for you, I want you to visualise it clearly. Imagine it as a red spinning energy, marking the direction of the movement. Once you've got this picture in your mind, here's the next step: speed it up. Double the speed of that red spinning motion, and as you do, you'll notice the anxiety intensifying. It's remarkable how easily we can make ourselves feel more anxious just by amplifying that sensation, by letting the spin accelerate. But here's the good news—just as you've sped it up, you can also slow it back down.

Gradually reduce the speed until the spin returns to its original pace. Already, you'll feel the anxiety settling. But let's take it further. Slow the spin even more—bring it down to half speed, then to a quarter. And then, stop it completely. Feel the stillness that follows when that anxious energy is absent.

Now, for the fun part: reverse the direction. Imagine that red spin turning green as it begins to rotate in the opposite direction. Let it start slowly, just as before—25%, then 50%, and finally back to full speed in the opposite direction. As it spins in this new way, notice how different you feel.

Keep thinking about the thing that used to make you anxious. The tension that was there earlier is dissipating. Where once there was anxiety, there is now something else and the opposite of anxiety is curiosity. And you can be curious about the sense of calm returning to the body. This is important because calm and curiosity are features of your safety repaired.

Now, bring to mind again the thing that was causing your anxiety. Look at it but notice how it's not the same as it was before. Something about the feeling has shifted, hasn't it? You've turned your fear around. Keep those green feeling spinning, reinforcing the new feeling of ease and control.

This technique isn't just about stopping anxiety—it's about expanding your understanding of what is possible in the *inner game*. You see, by engaging with the physical sensation of anxiety, by adjusting its speed and direction, you're showing yourself that this feeling is not as fixed or out of control at all. You *can* intervene. You are *able* alter it. You can speed it up, slow it down and put it into reverse. You have *agency*. You have *control!*

Now that you have the ability to think about things that used to scare you with complete impunity, I invite you to make a list of all of those things that once scared you. As you spin the green feeling, begin to grin as their effect on you floats out of you like vapour from a hot tub on a cool evening. The more you practice replacing unpleasant feelings with pleasant feelings the more you will, bit by bit, enjoy life to the fullest; which is the direction we are going now.

Let's explore these kinaesthetic submodalities in a technique designed to deepen the sense of calm inside you. The kind of inner calm that feels not only tranquil but also can be summoned at will—a practice I call *Wrapped in Serenity*. This technique not only helps to centre you in moments where you are under pressure but also teaches your body and mind to associate a simple gesture with profound peace. The beauty of this technique lies in its subtlety; the more you practice it, the more it becomes a natural part of your emotional toolkit, ready to be deployed whenever you need it.

WRAPPED in Serenity

As you spin the green feeling, begin at the back of your mind, to remember a time when you felt completely calm and tranquil and serene. This is not just a casual glimpse of a memory—rather, I want you to truly immerse yourself in it. Maybe it was a time you were on holiday, watching the mesmerising sheen of sunlight glistening the sea. Or maybe it was a time when you were enjoying a lovely massage, and you found your mind drifting somewhere between being awake and in a dream. Whatever is your memory, remember a moment when calmness enveloped you, when the world seemed to align in peaceful harmony, and you felt entirely in control.

Close your eyes. And allow yourself to drift back into that experience. What do you see around you? What are the sounds that fill the air? Can you smell tranquil scents? Everyone is as unique as their own thumb print, so when you have a serene experience, savour it and file it away for later use. For me, the time that I go back to is my first time in India with my (to be) wife.

I was lazing on a hammock between two coconut trees on an island, which had palest sand I had ever seen. The island was off the coast of Goa and was idyllic. The sun was the colour of an egg yoke, which crowned the azure blue sky. The warmth of that sun was perfectly balanced by cool of the sea breeze. The hammock swayed in the breeze and, with the sound of the sea, I closed my eyes. I could hear children laughing in the distance, sea birds nearby and I drifted off into a revery. That was over twenty years ago and I can conjure it back effortlessly.

Whatever your memory you can bring to mind, the most important thing is to pick one gives a deep sense of peacefulness. When the feeling comes, how does it *feel* to be in that state of calm? If a specific memory doesn't come to mind, don't worry. Simply imagine a scene where you are as relaxed as you could ever wish to be, fully equipped with ease, comfort, and an unshakeable sense of self-control. Now start to spin that feeling of serenity into the green feeling.

Now, as you settle into that memory or imagined scene, let's take it a step further. I want you to *enhance* the experience—begin to manipulate and play with your submodalities. Make the colours softer and more gentle and more lovely. Make the sounds more soothing, more melodic, more entrancing. Spin all of these changes into the green feeling and say inside your mind, '*soften*', and say it softer. Softest.

Let yourself be completely absorbed by this serenity as it spread through your whole body. As you do this, gently press the thumb and middle finger of your right hand together. This is an important part of the technique, as it creates a physical link to this calm feeling: *things that are fired together are wired together*. By repeating this simple gesture while immersed in serenity, you're teaching your mind and body that this sensation of calm is always accessible. Do this a few times, each time deepening the peace you feel.

Now, let's solidify this connection. Reloop that moment of calm at least five more times. Each time you revisit it, spin the green feeling, press your thumb and middle finger together, reinforcing the bond between this gentle action and the serene emotions. You'll know the technique is taking effect when, simply by squeezing your thumb and finger, you start to feel a gentle wave of relaxation washing over you.

Next, we'll move on to a scenario that has caused you mild stress in the past. Think of a situation that, while not overwhelming, has triggered some level of tension or unease. As you bring that situation to mind, spinning the calm feeling, press your thumb and middle finger together once again. Let the calming sensation flow through you. Welcome that feeling. Now, see yourself carrying this calm into the stressful situation. As you spin the calm feeling, visualise everything unfolding smoothly, just as you would want it to. See the scene before you, hear the sounds, and feel what it is like to feel so safe, to remain calm and composed.

With that sense of calm fully restored, let's up the challenge. While continuing to press your thumb and finger together, think of the same scenario, but this time add a few extra challenges or obstacles. Perhaps the stakes are higher, or the demands on you are greater. But here's the key—spin the calming feeling, press your thumb and finger together, and see yourself handling it all with ease. Picture yourself moving through the scene with the same serenity as before. Hear the sounds, feel the sensations, and enjoy the satisfaction of knowing that no matter what arises, you remain in control.

Now, take a moment of quiet reflection. Notice the change in how you feel about what used to be a stressful situation. It is no longer daunting, is it? Practice is an important feature of this ability. These things are never 'one and done'. Repeat the exercise regularly so that, should you be blindsided by an event or a moment, you'll know how to restore a sense of calm both consciously and unconsciously. With each repetition, you'll find that spinning feelings of calm becomes easier and more immediate. The control is at your fingertips.

Through this practice, you are not only building a reliable way to reduce stress; you are training your mind and body to work together, creating a sense of calm that you can summon whenever you need it most. This is the power of *Wrapped in Serenity*—simple, subtle, and yet deeply transformative.

As we conclude our exploration of instinct in leadership, remember that developing instinctual intelligence and effective stress management is an ongoing journey. It requires consistent practice, reflection, and a willingness to learn from both successes and failures. By mastering their *inner game*, leaders can navigate the complexities of business with greater confidence, agility, and effectiveness, while also creating more resilient and psychologically safe work environments.

SECTION TWO SUMMARY

*I can be changed by what happens to me.
But I refuse to be reduced by it*
Maya Angelou

The Personal Resilience Skills part serves as the foundation for mastering *neuro-resilience*, equipping leaders with the tools to navigate stress, regulate emotions, and enhance their decision-making. By delving into the interplay between instinct, physiology, and cognition, this part provides a practical framework for understanding and transforming unconscious responses into conscious, productive behaviours.

The journey began with Core Skills in Chapter 4, where readers are introduced to the fundamental concept of instinct mapping. Drawing parallels between the instinctive responses of humans and animals, such as a gazelle's fight-or-flight reactions, the chapter explores how these primal patterns manifest in the workplace. Leaders learn that their body often chooses its responses—mobilisation, immobilisation, or social engagement—before the conscious mind even registers the situation[1]. Through techniques like Instinct Mapping and Finding Home, readers gain the ability to uncover their unique sensory patterns and regulate stress responses, setting the stage for more intentional and informed actions.

In Chapter 5, Intermediate Skills expands on these foundations, equipping readers with methods to manage more complex and emotionally charged situations. Leaders learn to maintain balance and perspective, even under significant pressure, by recognising the physiological and emotional triggers that can derail their effectiveness. Techniques such as Stepping Out of Fear, Taming Vicious Memories, and Silencing the Storm help leaders reframe their experiences, transforming overwhelming emotions into manageable challenges. Silencing the Storm, in particular, teaches leaders to dismantle internal narratives of self-doubt and worry, replacing them with constructive inner dialogues that restore emotional balance.

Finally, Advanced Skills in Chapter 6 takes readers to the next level of neuro-resilience mastery, introducing techniques to fine-tune emotional regulation and deepen instinctual intelligence. Leaders learn to move beyond instinct awareness into instinct acuity and intelligence, developing the ability to not only recognise but also manipulate and transform their emotional states. Techniques like Turning Anxiety Around and Wrapped in Serenity empower leaders to proactively reshape negative emotions, using them as opportunities for growth and self-mastery. This chapter also introduces the concept of layering calmness into even the most challenging situations, creating a reservoir of resilience that leaders can draw upon whenever needed.

Across all three chapters, the emphasis is on practice, reflection, and refinement. Leaders are encouraged to embrace these tools as lifelong skills, essential not only for personal growth but also for creating resilient, psychologically safe environments for their teams. By the end of this part, readers will have gained a robust toolkit for navigating the complexities of leadership with confidence, clarity, and calm.

Techniques Introduced in Part 2[2]:

1. **Instinct Mapping** – Identify sensory patterns of primal responses.
2. **Finding Home** – Reset emotional balance to return to a state of calm.
3. **Stepping Out of Fear** – Create distance and clarity from overwhelming thoughts.
4. **Taming Vicious Memories** – Reframe emotionally charged past experiences.
5. **Silencing the Storm** – Dial down the negative internal dialogue.
6. **Turning Anxiety Around** – Reverse the physical sensations of anxiety.
7. **Wrapped in Serenity** – Anchor sweet calmness through kinaesthetic.

These techniques collectively form the foundation of personal resilience, enabling leaders to transform their instinctual responses into tools for success and wellbeing.

SECTION TWO SUMMARY

Autoregulation Exercises

Instinct Mapping

<u>Step 1: Choose Two Instincts to Explore</u>

Think of one "move towards" instinctual response that are pleasure seeking (such as desire, lust, or ambition) and one "move away from" response that you strongly dislike (such as disgust, fear, or rage). Write them down ahead of time.

<u>Step 2: Recreate the Positive Instinct</u>

Close your eyes and summon a vivid memory of a time when you felt the "move towards" instinct deeply, like a strong desire or lust. Bring the memory to life by seeing what you saw, hearing what you heard, and feeling what you felt.

<u>Step 3: Record the Negative Submodalities</u>

Using the 'Experience 1' column in the *Submodality Comparisons* sheet below, itemise the characteristics and qualities for each sensory modality.

<u>Step 4: Recreate the Positive Instinct</u>

Next, bring up a memory of the "move away from" instinct. Recreate the strong negative feeling, whether it was fear, disgust, or anger, and re-live it fully, with the same intensity as you experienced in the moment.

<u>Step 5: Record the Negative Submodalities</u>

Using the 'Experience 2' column in the *Submodality Comparisons* sheet below, itemise the characteristics and qualities for each sensory modality.

<u>Step 6: Compare the Differences</u>

Now compare the submodalities of your two instincts. What are the main differences between how you experienced the "move towards" and the "move away from" responses?

As Richard Bandler states, "It's the differences that make the difference". So, look for differences, not what's similar. That way you can easily calibrate to how your brain codes the positive versus the negative instinct.

Submodality Comparison Sheet

	Experience 1	Experience 2
VISUAL		
Number of images		
Motion/still		
Colour/black and white		
Bright/dim		
Focused/unfocused		
Bordered/panoramic		
Associated/dissociated		
Centre-weighted/wide angle		
Size (relative to life)		
Shape Three-dimensional/flat		
Close/distant		
Location in space		
AUDITORY		
Number of sounds/sources		
Volume		
Tone		
Tempo		
Pitch		
Pace		
Timber		
Duration		
Intensity		
Direction		
Intensity		
Direction		
Rhythm		
Harmony		
More in one ear than another		
KINESTHETIC		
Location in body		
Breathing rate		
Pulse rate		
Skin temperature		
Weight		
Pressure		
Intensity		
Tactile sensations		
OLFACTORY & GUSTATORY		
Sweet		
Sour		
Salt		
Bitter		
Aroma		
Fragrance		
Essences		
Pungence		

SECTION TWO SUMMARY

Submodality Comparison Sheet

	Experience 1	Experience 2
VISUAL		
Number of images		
Motion/still		
Colour/black and white		
Bright/dim		
Focused/unfocused		
Bordered/panoramic		
Associated/dissociated		
Centre-weighted/wide angle		
Size (relative to life)		
Shape Three-dimensional/flat		
Close/distant		
Location in space		
AUDITORY		
Number of sounds/sources		
Volume		
Tone		
Tempo		
Pitch		
Pace		
Timber		
Duration		
Intensity		
Direction		
Intensity		
Direction		
Rhythm		
Harmony		
More in one ear than another		
KINESTHETIC		
Location in body		
Breathing rate		
Pulse rate		
Skin temperature		
Weight		
Pressure		
Intensity		
Tactile sensations		
OLFACTORY & GUSTATORY		
Sweet		
Sour		
Salt		
Bitter		
Aroma		
Fragrance		
Essences		
Pungence		

Submodality Comparison Sheet

	Experience 1	Experience 2
VISUAL		
Number of images		
Motion/still		
Colour/black and white		
Bright/dim		
Focused/unfocused		
Bordered/panoramic		
Associated/dissociated		
Centre-weighted/wide angle		
Size (relative to life)		
Shape Three-dimensional/flat		
Close/distant		
Location in space		
AUDITORY		
Number of sounds/sources		
Volume		
Tone		
Tempo		
Pitch		
Pace		
Timber		
Duration		
Intensity		
Direction		
Intensity		
Direction		
Rhythm		
Harmony		
More in one ear than another		
KINESTHETIC		
Location in body		
Breathing rate		
Pulse rate		
Skin temperature		
Weight		
Pressure		
Intensity		
Tactile sensations		
OLFACTORY & GUSTATORY		
Sweet		
Sour		
Salt		
Bitter		
Aroma		
Fragrance		
Essences		
Pungence		

SECTION TWO SUMMARY

Submodality Comparison Sheet

	Experience 1	Experience 2
VISUAL		
Number of images		
Motion/still		
Colour/black and white		
Bright/dim		
Focused/unfocused		
Bordered/panoramic		
Associated/dissociated		
Centre-weighted/wide angle		
Size (relative to life)		
Shape Three-dimensional/flat		
Close/distant		
Location in space		
AUDITORY		
Number of sounds/sources		
Volume		
Tone		
Tempo		
Pitch		
Pace		
Timber		
Duration		
Intensity		
Direction		
Intensity		
Direction		
Rhythm		
Harmony		
More in one ear than another		
KINESTHETIC		
Location in body		
Breathing rate		
Pulse rate		
Skin temperature		
Weight		
Pressure		
Intensity		
Tactile sensations		
OLFACTORY & GUSTATORY		
Sweet		
Sour		
Salt		
Bitter		
Aroma		
Fragrance		
Essences		
Pungence		

Finding Home

Goal: To manage stress through a calm and controlled mindset.

1. Take a moment to think about the five biggest sources of stress in your life right now.

- Write them down. Naming your stressors makes them easier to handle.

2. Choose one stressor from your list to focus on for this exercise.

3. Activate Your *Finding Home Again* anchor

- Use a physical gesture (such as pressing your thumb and finger together) to signal calmness.
- Take a deep, steady breath while doing this to centre yourself.

4. Bring the stressful situation to mind but imagine yourself handling it with complete calmness.

- Picture yourself moving through the situation smoothly and effortlessly.
- See what you'll see, hear the sounds around you, and feel the calm in your body.

5. Now, imagine the situation with some challenges or setbacks.

- Visualise yourself calmly handling these challenges with the same ease and control.

- Keep your physical anchor gesture active to maintain your calm state.

6. Pause and check in with yourself. How do you feel about that stressor now?

- Notice if your body feels more relaxed or if the stressor feels less intense.

7. Move on to the other stressors on your list, repeating steps 2 to 6 for each one.

- Take your time, allowing the calm feeling to settle in after each round.

8. Build Long-Term Calm

- With practice, your mind will learn to handle stress from a place of calm and resilience.
- Over time, your unconscious mind will make this state your new default, helping you handle future stress more easily.

Practice this exercise regularly to make calmness a natural part of your response to life's challenges.

Stepping out of Fear

1. Identify the Stressor

   - Recall the stressful situation-past, present, or future.
   - Picture it clearly, either as a still image or a short video.

2. Step Out of the Scene

   - Imagine watching yourself in the scene, as if it's a film.
   - Visualise floating back until you can see the back of your own head.
   - Keep moving away until the scene is about three metres distant.

3. Create Emotional Distance

   - Turn the image black and white-this dulls its intensity.
   - Shrink the image to a tenth of its original size, making it feel smaller.
   - Make it transparent - let it fade until it's barely there.

4. Observe the Shift

   - Notice how the emotional weight has lightened.
   - You can now see the situation with greater calmness and objectivity.
   - This method helps disengage from overwhelming emotions, allowing you to regain clarity and control.

With the emotional intensity reduced, ask yourself if there are any decisions you need to make regarding the situation. If so, make those decisions from this calmer, more detached viewpoint.

Taming Vicious Memories

1. Sit in a cozy, relaxing space where you feel safe and comfortable. Imagine you're sitting in a peaceful cinema, ready to watch a movie.
2. Picture yourself in a comfy chair, with the lights dimmed, and everything quiet. You're fully relaxed, about to watch a film.
3. Imagine you gently float out of your seat and rise towards the projection booth above. From there, you can see yourself below, seated comfortably, watching the screen.
4. Think of a troubling memory. Identify two key moments:
   - The **Before Moment** (just before the difficult event happened).
   - The **After Moment** (right after the event has passed, when you're safe).
5. From your safe spot in the projection booth, see yourself in the cinema, watching the **Before Moment** projected on the screen.
6. Watch the memory unfold on the screen, moving from the **Before Moment** to the **After Moment**. Once it ends, freeze the scene at the **After Moment**, where you're safe.
7. Now, in your mind, rewind the memory quickly, from the end back to the start. Watch it all unravel in reverse. Repeat this step **three times**.
8. Each time you rewind the memory, observe how its emotional intensity lessens. The memory will start to feel more distant, like watching a movie instead of reliving it.
9. After the process, recall the memory. If you can remember it without the strong emotional charge, the exercise has been effective.
10. To further reduce any lingering discomfort, engage in

regular relaxation practices, like listening to calming music or a guided meditation. This helps reinforce the change.

By regularly practicing this exercise, you can reframe difficult memories, reducing their emotional weight and gaining clarity and peace.

Wrapped In Serenity

1. **Recall a Calm Memory**
   - Close your eyes.
   - Think of a time when you felt completely serene and at peace.
   - Imagine what you saw, heard, and felt in that moment of calm.
   - If no specific memory comes to mind, create a peaceful scene in your imagination where you feel totally relaxed.

2. **Deepen the Experience**
   - Enhance that memory or imagined scene: make the colours brighter, the sounds clearer, and the feelings stronger.
   - As you do this, gently press your thumb and middle finger together on your right hand. This will create a physical connection to the feeling of calm.

3. **Repeat to Reinforce**
   - Replay the calm memory or scene in your mind at least five times.
   - Each time, press your thumb and middle finger together again, strengthening the link between the gesture and the feeling of serenity.
   - Over time, this gesture will help trigger calmness more easily.

4. **Apply to a Mildly Stressful Situation**
   - Think of a situation that caused you mild stress in the past.
   - As you recall it, press your thumb and middle finger together.

- Imagine yourself feeling calm and in control during that situation, just as you did in your serene memory. Visualise it unfolding smoothly.

5. **Add Challenges**
    - Now think of the same stressful situation but add a few more challenges to it—perhaps the stakes are higher, or the pressure is greater.
    - While pressing your thumb and middle finger together, imagine yourself handling these new challenges with the same serenity and control.

6. **Reflect and Repeat**
    - Take a moment to reflect. Do you feel calmer and in control about the stressful situation?
    - If not, repeat the exercise until accessing your sense of calm becomes easier and more immediate.

This technique will help you build a reliable, calming tool to reduce stress and maintain control in challenging situations

PART THREE
REPAIR & PREVENT TRAUMA

INTRODUCTION

I have been impressed with the urgency of doing.
Knowing is not enough; we must apply.
Being willing is not enough; we must do.
Leonardo da Vinci

The aim of *Part Two* was to lay the foundations for understanding the particulars of your own human stress responses, their evolutionary origins, and the neuro-resilient techniques that equip individuals to navigate life's challenges. In this part, we move from foundational principles to practical application, exploring how neuro-resilience manifests in real-world contexts—particularly when the stakes are high, emotions run deep, and safety is ruptured.

This part is not merely theoretical; it delves into the complexities of human experience, addressing what happens when safety—both psychological and emotional—is compromised. The chapters present practical strategies to address these challenges, repair the damage, and prevent future occurrences. As you engage with these chapters, you'll find yourself stepping into vivid scenarios and transformative dialogues, learning techniques that can be applied to your own life and leadership.

In Chapter 7: *When Safety is Ruptured*, we witness Jerry's breakdown in a high-pressure mining operation. His story illustrates the profound impact of unmanaged stress on both individuals and teams. Through Jerry's "frozen" state, we see how modern stressors—though vastly different from the dangers of our evolutionary past—trigger the same primal responses, leading to immobilisation, disconnection, and eventual collapse. Jerry's experience highlights the urgency for leaders to recognise and intervene before stress spirals into trauma. This chapter explores the nature of psychological safety, its fragility, and the critical role of neuro-resilient practices in recovery and repair.

Moving forward, Chapter 8: *Rupture Repair Coaching* provides a detailed, immersive look into the repair process. Through a facilitated coaching session, I help Jerry regain his sense of calm and control. The session is a testament to the power of rapport, humour, and neuro-resilient techniques such as *Turning Anxiety Around* and *Wrapped in Serenity* techniques. It demonstrates how a skilled practitioner can guide an individual from distress to empowerment, equipping them with lasting tools for emotional regulation. This chapter is a practical guide for coaches, leaders, and anyone seeking to support others through periods of acute stress or trauma.

Finally, Chapter 9: *Rupture Prevention Practices* shifts focus to the preventative measures that can fortify individuals against the accumulation of stress. This chapter champions the adage, "An ounce of prevention is worth a pound of cure," emphasising the importance of daily autoregulation routines and mindful rituals. Whether through morning practices that energise and ground or nighttime routines that invite restorative sleep, readers will learn how to proactively cultivate resilience. The techniques discussed here are simple yet profound, encouraging consistency and intentionality to prevent safety ruptures from occurring in the first place.

Throughout this part, the emphasis is clear: neuro-resilience is not just about recovery; it is about creating environments—both internal and external—that foster safety, connection, and sustainable well-being. Whether you are leading a team, coaching an individual, or striving for personal growth, the lessons and techniques in these chapters will equip you to meet life's challenges with composure, creativity, and confidence.

As you read, consider how the scenarios and solutions resonate with your own experiences. Reflect on the ways safety has been compromised in your life or work and how the techniques presented here might help you rebuild or reinforce it. These are advanced skills for a reason—they go beyond basic stress management to address the deeper layers of human resilience, enabling not just survival, but flourishing. By the end of this part, you will not only understand these skills but be ready to apply them, transforming your approach to stress, safety, and success.

SEVEN
WHEN SAFETY IS RUPTURED

> *You'll be caught in the middle of the madness*
> *Just lost like them, part of all the pain they feel*
> **Ronnie James Dio**

RED DESERT DISTRESS: Picture a mining operation in the middle of Australia. The landscape is both bleak and beautiful, dominated by red-hued earth, towering piles of processed ore, and large earth-moving vehicles steadily working in the heat. Despite the scorching sun, the workers wear hard hats, thick leather gloves, Hi-Viz vests, and reinforced boots. The operation runs like clockwork, with workers flying in and out on a tight schedule. This is routine.

Then suddenly, a crack appears in that routine. Jerry, the *Head of Engineering*, is meant to catch the flight out at the end of his shift, but instead, he refuses to leave. His colleagues buzz with curiosity and mild amusement as they board the plane without him, but the site *General Manager*, Douglas, senses something deeper is wrong.

Walking into Jerry's office, Douglas finds him frozen in place, eyes wide, teeth clenched in a terrified grimace, sweat dripping down his face, gripping his desk as though it's the only thing tethering him to reality.

Jerry has hit a breaking point, but this isn't just a moment of frustration or anger. It's a profound loss of emotional safety—a sudden stress response known as *freeze*[1]. In that moment, Jerry is incapable of social engagement or rational decision-making. His nervous system, unable to reconcile the pressures he's been facing, has shut down. To understand what's happening to Jerry, we need to delve deeper into the human stress response—an ancient mechanism that once ensured our ancestors' survival but can now wreak havoc in contemporary workplaces.

Jerry's frozen state, marked by a blend of heightened metabolism and immobilised action, is a natural, if not entirely helpful, response to overwhelming stress. In evolutionary terms, it's the same instinct that would have caused our ancestors to freeze at the sight of a predator lurking in the shadows, hoping to remain unnoticed and thus avoid danger.

Today, however, the perceived threats aren't sabre-toothed tigers but professional failures, economic insecurity, or the looming possibility of job loss. Yet to Jerry's reptilian brain, the distinction is irrelevant[2]. It reacts as though his survival is at stake, flooding his body with cortisol, freezing his muscles, and shutting down his capacity for social interaction.

As we've already explored in earlier chapters, the human stress response isn't limited to *fight* or *flight*—it also includes *freeze* and *shutdown*. When Jerry's body reaches the tipping point of stress, it defaults to freeze, paralysing his decision-making and social faculties. This could have been mitigated if Jerry had practised techniques like *Finding Home*, a neuro-resilience method designed to help individuals reset their emotional and physiological balance before reaching a breaking point. By regularly recalibrating his nervous system, Jerry could have prevented the slow build-up of stress that eventually led to this collapse.

EVOLUTIONARY ORIGINS

> *Stress is like fire.*
> *It can keep you warm, or it can burn you.*
> *It's all about how you handle it.*
> **Richard Bandler**

To understand how Jerry's modern-day crisis mirrors ancient survival instincts, we need to take a step back and consider how the stress response evolved. Picture our ancestors huddled around a fire, hyper-aware of the dangers lurking in the wilderness. A sudden snap of a twig in the distance would send hearts racing and minds scrambling, preparing the group for either confrontation or escape. This acute stress response was essential for survival.

Fast forward to today, and while the dangers have changed, the brain's response has not. The human brain, particularly the limbic system, is hardwired to detect threats to our safety—whether physical, social, or psychological. In the modern workplace, threats to job security, status, or professional reputation can trigger the same neurobiological reactions as life-or-death situations. When leaders and employees lack the skills to recognise and manage these responses, chronic stress can quickly take over, leading to burnout, disengagement, or, in Jerry's case, trauma.

In earlier chapters, we discussed *Instinct Mapping*, a method leaders can use to identify stress triggers in themselves and their teams. Douglas, the site manager, could have employed this technique to become more aware of Jerry's rising stress levels before they reached a critical point. Recognising the warning signs—such as irritability, reduced focus, and increasing withdrawal—could have prompted an earlier intervention, giving Jerry the support he needed to regulate his stress.

Workplace Wellbeing

> *Your brain has a fantastic capacity for stress, but it's equally capable of creating calm and joy. Choose your focus.*[3]
> **Richard Bandler**

CHRONIC STRESS IS NOT only debilitating for the individual; it creates ripple effects throughout a team or organisation. In Jerry's case, his stress-induced breakdown doesn't just affect his own performance; it influences everyone around him. His irritability, poor focus, and declining problem-solving abilities are felt by his colleagues, increasing their own stress levels and disrupting the flow of work.

In organisations where safety is fragile or non-existent, stress spreads like a virus. As Jerry's condition deteriorates, he begins micromanaging his team, driven by a hypervigilant need to regain control. This, in turn, stifles his colleagues' creativity and autonomy. Tasks are delayed, tensions rise, and eventually, the entire team's productivity suffers. This is the cost of unmanaged stress.

This is where techniques like *Stepping Out of Fear*, which we covered in Chapter 5, become crucial. Leaders like Douglas can learn to confront their own fears about difficult conversations or performance failures, allowing them to better address the stress in their teams. By stepping out of fear, leaders can prevent small issues from spiralling into full-blown crises, much like the one Jerry is experiencing.

Occupational Trauma

> *People aren't broken.*
> *They just have strategies that aren't working,*
> *causing them unnecessary distress.*
> **Richard Bandler**

As the site manager, Douglas plays a pivotal role in either exacerbating or alleviating Jerry's stress. His response in the office, when he finds Jerry frozen in fear, is critical. In Chapter 8, we introduced the concept of *co-regulation*, where individuals in a group unconsciously regulate their emotional states based on the signals they receive from others. In this case, if Douglas approaches Jerry with calm, open body language, and a regulated emotional state, he can help Jerry down-regulate his own stress response.

Had Douglas been more in tune with his own emotional regulation, he might have been able to guide Jerry back to a state of psychological safety. In earlier chapters, we discussed the importance of *Taming Vicious Memories*, a technique that helps individuals prevent past fears or failures from influencing their present state.

This technique, applied both by leaders and their teams, can prevent past mistakes or challenges from escalating into debilitating stress. If Jerry and Douglas had worked through previous project setbacks with this mindset, the situation might have played out differently.

Psychological safety, once ruptured, can be challenging to repair. The good news is that skilled practitioners using the right techniques can repair trauma quickly. After Jerry's breakdown, Douglas must take deliberate steps to restore trust and safety within the team. First, he arranges Jerry to meet with a coach to restore his lost safety, the transcript of which we cover in the next chapter.

Second, he brought the whole of site together to address the matter, which is delved into in *'The Outer Game of Leadership'* to begin a new phase for the mine site. This includes dialogues where team members can express their concerns without fear of judgement, structured feedback sessions, or even team-building activities designed to reconnect the group.

By implementing regular check-ins, debriefs, or shared relaxation practices, Douglas helps his team re-establish a sense of safety and cohesion. These rituals allow team members to process their stress collectively, reducing the likelihood of future breakdowns.

Leaders must also practice *Active Hearing*, ensuring that team members feel heard and valued, especially after a stressful event. When team members see that their concerns are taken seriously and acted upon, they're more likely to trust the process of rebuilding psychological safety.

Jerry's breakdown serves as a cautionary tale, not just about the dangers of unmanaged stress but about the importance of proactive, neuro-resilient leadership. Leaders like Douglas must be equipped with the skills to recognise the signs of stress in themselves and their teams and to intervene before it's too late. By practising neuro-resilient techniques, such as *Instinct Mapping*, *Stepping Out of Fear*, and *Taming Vicious Memories*, leaders can help create environments where stress is managed, and psychological safety is maintained.

Rebuilding safety after a breakdown takes some effort, but it can be done well. By focusing on co-regulation, empathetic communication, and team rituals, leaders can help their teams bounce back stronger and more resilient than before. In the end, it's the leader's ability to navigate stress—both their own and their team's—that determines the success or failure of the entire organisation.

Chronic stress doesn't just stay at the level of unease or discomfort—it can spiral into something far more destructive: occupational trauma.

This is where we begin to encounter the long-term effects of unmanaged stress, particularly in fast-paced, high-stakes environments.

Occupational trauma isn't limited to catastrophic events like accidents or violence in the workplace. It also emerges from a series of small, insidious stressors—deadlines that never seem to relent, public criticism, and the looming fear of job loss or failure. These everyday stressors accumulate, chipping away at the individual's resilience until they face total collapse.

Let's return to the 'Jerry Moment': his immobilisation in the office wasn't an isolated incident; it was the product of months, perhaps even years, of eroded safety and unchecked stress. Like a cliff gradually eroded by unrelenting waves, Jerry's capacity to cope was worn thin by the constant barrage of work pressures. At some point, the weight of the stress became too much, and the collapse happened. Jerry's line manager, Douglas, had been 'caught in the middle of the madness' too, he had been disoriented too, just like Jerry, and part of the all pain the entire mine site was feeling.

This phenomenon is echoed in the brain's neuroplasticity, where repetitive exposure to stress strengthens neural pathways associated with fear and anxiety. This rewiring makes individuals more susceptible to triggering stress reactions, and over time, they lose access to their higher-order thinking, decision-making, and emotional regulation abilities. It's as though the brain itself becomes trapped in survival mode, perpetuating a cycle of stress responses.

When high alert becomes chronic, it leads to a state of near-constant mobilisation. Once the human body is shunted into flight-or-flight, the human brain loses a load of cognitive heft. By some measures, that can be as much as 35%. This heightened fight-or-flight state becomes more dangerous the longer it is sustained, transforming what was once an adaptive survival response into something destructive—burnout, anxiety disorders, and even depression.

Now, we see a new side of the survival response. What happens when someone like Jerry is unable to escape their work environment? The constant stress means that the brain's mobilisation response is no longer enough to handle the strain, and the nervous system turns to immobilisation. This is the classic *freeze* response—the body goes rigid, physically unable to engage with the situation anymore.

The issue with chronic mobilisation and immobilisation is that these responses shut down creativity, engagement, and communication—core elements of any successful team. As Jerry becomes more disconnected and anxious, the more isolated he becomes from his peers, his family, and even himself. What happens next? Depression, anxiety, and withdrawal.

Trauma-Informed Leading

A frozen leader can't lead, and a frozen team can't perform. This is how chronic stress can not only destroy the individual but corrode the culture of an entire organisation.

Here's where the role of leadership becomes crucial. Trauma-informed leadership is not a new management theory—it's an approach that recognises the reality of occupational trauma. Leaders in this position need to become adept at spotting the subtle signs of chronic stress before it tips into trauma, and they need to know how to foster an environment that heals rather than exacerbates these stresses.

Key principles of trauma-informed leadership include:

1. *Normalising Conversations on Mental Health*: Rather than treating stress or emotional strain as isolated issues, normalise discussions around them, encouraging employees to seek help when needed.

2. *Recognising Stress in Real-Time:* Leaders should be trained to detect early warning signs—tension in the room, short tempers, silence during meetings—and intervene before stress spirals out of control.
3. *Preventing Burnout with Boundaries:* Create systems that allow people to recharge. This includes work-life balance policies, adequate leave, and encouraging employees to step back when they need to.
4. *Modelling Emotional Regulation:* Leaders themselves should be emotionally aware and demonstrate emotional resilience, helping to co-regulate the emotional states of their teams.

This type of leadership isn't just about managing crises; it's about proactively cultivating resilience in the workplace and ensuring that chronic stress doesn't lead to occupational trauma.

But what happens if this culture of psychological safety is lost? What if chronic stress has already taken root in your organisation? As we transition to Part Three, we will delve into the steps leaders can take to *repair* this damage.

The next chapter will begin by demonstrating *PACE Protocol* and *Safety Priming*, advanced co-regulation skillset that supports coaches and leaders can use to ruptured safety.

EIGHT
RUPTURE REPAIR COACHING

If you can't laugh at your past, you'll never get free of it. So it's time to start laughing, even if it's artificial laughter at first[1].
Richard Bandler

JERRY'S TRAUMA from his workplace challenges and the toll it took on his mental and emotional well-being, was explored in Chapter 7. His struggles were compounded by a cycle of anxiety and self-doubt, often triggered by specific work-related scenarios.

Now, in Chapter 8, we delve deeper into the process of recovery, focusing on practical coaching methods to repair emotional ruptures and restore a sense of personal agency. Below is a transcript of a coaching session I had with Jerry, during which he was grappling with the aftermath of his 'freeze' moment.

Helping people recover from trauma requires guiding their subjective experiences to produce a measurable effect on their biology—specifically, their metabolism. When people are in a state of trauma, their metabolism becomes misaligned with their environment. Therefore, the primary goal is clear:

Resynchronise their metabolism with their actual environment.

Practitioners achieve this through *Safety Priming* and coaching participants to regulate their own subjective experiences. By understanding how external and internal stimuli impact the brain and body, we can more effectively navigate their emotional landscape.

This process is similar to how a chef crafts a culinary masterpiece. A chef combines various temperatures, cooking times, and ingredients in precise ways to transform raw elements into an extraordinary meal. Understanding the science behind how heat and chemistry interact with ingredients allows the chef to create dishes that not only taste exceptional but also evoke specific physiological responses in their patrons[2].

A chef deliberately crafts a multisensory experience designed to produce measurable effects on a customer's biology:

- **Heightened Sensory Stimulation:** Vivid presentation, rich aromas, and complex textures intensely activate the limbic system, boosting dopamine, deepening anticipation, and priming the body for digestion.
- **Enhanced Pleasure & Reward:** Unique flavours and gourmet ingredients provoke stronger dopamine and endorphin release, intensifying satisfaction. Spices and umami-rich foods amplify pleasure and emotional fulfilment.
- **Optimised Satiety & Metabolism:** High-quality fats and proteins trigger more cholecystokinin (CCK) and leptin, deepening satiety, increasing thermogenesis, and boosting metabolism.
- **Deep Relaxation & Elevated Mood:** Post-meal, elevated serotonin and oxytocin promote calm energy and emotional well-being.

In sum, a chef's masterpiece transforms eating into a full-body experience of sensory pleasure, metabolic balance, and emotional fulfilment. Similarly, Neuro-Linguistic Programming (NLP) techniques aim to influence a person's subjective experience to produce measurable effects on their objective biology. Once this synchronisation is achieved, the participant naturally shifts their mental and physical behaviour.

For leaders and coaches, the 'ingredients and seasoning' are delivered through vocal prosody, sensory acuity, somatic awareness, wordplay, humour, and other co-regulatory techniques—each carefully calibrated to build trust, safety, and resilient change. By doing so, leaders use their neurology and skills as resources to help people move from a disconnected state to a grounded calm and optimistic one.

The PACE Protocol

From the earliest days of my NLP journey, I found myself working with leaders at every level, helping them navigate ruptured safety within their organisations. These weren't therapy sessions, nor were they meant to be. They were leadership and coaching conversations —designed to sharpen focus, strengthen decision-making, and build resilience.

But here's the problem. The more senior the client, the more circuitous the conversations became. Not because of intellectual difficulties—leaders are more than capable of juggling different perspectives, strategies, and persuasion techniques. No, the real reason these conversations meandered was avoidance. Beneath the surface-level discussions of tactics and execution lay deeper, unspoken tensions— anger, anxiety, and, in some cases, apathy.

I would sometimes catch myself thinking,

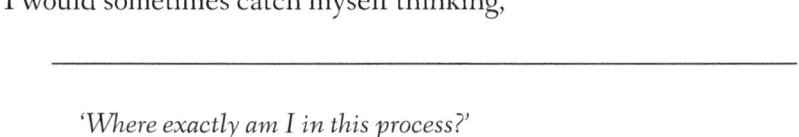

'Where exactly am I in this process?'

Richard Bandler never seemed to have this problem. I'd spent hours training with him and watching his demonstrations—both live and on video. Of course, our contexts were different. He had the advantage of a controlled setting, a primed audience, and a chosen demonstration subject. Meanwhile, I worked with whoever walked in, with whatever baggage they brought.

And yet, despite all the tangents, the storytelling, the unexpected detours—Bandler never lost track of where he was, nor where he was going. His demonstration subjects had no idea where he was leading them, yet they followed.

So I shifted my focus. Instead of asking, *'What is he doing now?'*—because he was doing a lot simultaneously, and trying to track every move was like *unscrambling a scrambled egg*—I began looking for the underlying structure that kept everything cohesive.

It wasn't about deconstructing each movement, just as you can't unmix an omelette back into its individual eggs. It was about recognising *the rhythm that held it all together*. Or, to put it another way, watching Bandler work was like listening to a master jazz musician. On the surface, it was all improvisation—unexpected notes, unpredictable shifts, playful deviations[3].

But jazz isn't just noise. Beneath the apparent chaos, there's a *hidden structure—a time signature, a harmonic foundation, a sense of progression* that holds everything in place. The real skill isn't in following each note but in sensing the *invisible thread that pulls the whole piece forward*.

Once I started listening for that thread instead of trying to decode every individual moment, I realised something: it wasn't about tracking *what* he was doing; it was about tracking where he was leading them and what route he was taking.

So, I decided to ask a more straightforward questions:

'To where is he leading them?'

'Where is he going next?'

That shift in perspective led me to a simple but invaluable framework —one that provided structure without rigidity, direction without force. I called it the *PACE Protocol*, named after the 'pacing' technique from NLP.

At its core, *PACE* provides a map and compass for coaching conversations—particularly those involving safety ruptures, resistance, or deep-seated emotional blocks. It ensures that, no matter how unpredictable or circuitous the dialogue becomes, I always know *towards which direction I am moving*. More importantly, it allows me to stay fully present—attuned to the client's words, tone, and body language—without becoming lost in the complexity of the moment.

The **PACE Protocol** unfolds in four natural phases:

1. **Permission** – This is where trust is built, tension is defused, and the client feels safe enough to engage. I use a blend of observational, conversational, and behavioural NLP techniques, aka 'safety priming', which I explore in detail in *'The Outer Game of Leadership'*. Once trust is established, I begin testing for psychological permission—*probing* through teasing, humour, confronting questions, and other approaches.
2. **Agency** – The client already has control; they just don't realise it yet. My role is to surface that latent control, guiding their cognition to engage with their instinctual patterns of protection and deliberately alter them, reasserting their personal agency.
3. **Connection** – As they begin to regulate emotionally, their body and mind transition from protection to connection patterns. The telltale sign? Their humour returns. Playful back-and-forth banter signals safety—not just with me, but within themselves.
4. **Embedding**– Change must extend beyond the session; the client needs to feel safe *anywhere* and with *anyone*. Through repetition and reframing the new strategies and meanings are installed; and through *future pacing*, they vividly envision and explain how they will apply their new

patterns in real-world situations, ensuring lasting transformation.

These phases are not rigid steps but a dynamic flow, allowing for flexibility while maintaining direction. If a conversation takes an unexpected turn, the framework acts as a signpost rather than a constraint.

The beauty of this approach is that it allows *freedom within a framework*. It enables me to play with storytelling, analogies, and tangents, without ever losing track of the underlying trajectory. The coaching process remains fluid and responsive yet steadily progresses towards genuine change.

For leaders and coaches, this structured yet adaptive method offers a powerful tool—one that helps individuals reconnect with their inner resilience and take ownership of their own transformation.

Little Things Done Well

> *'Perfection' is just a lot of little things done well*
> **Chef Marco Pierre White**

How can leaders repair safety ruptures as thoughtfully as a master chef crafts a perfect meal? Just as Marco Pierre White suggests, achieving excellence is about consistently getting the small things right. The same principle applies to developing neuro-resilience skills—perfection is simply the result of many small, well-executed actions.

In the session, pay close attention to vocal tone, humour, pacing, and attentive listening. These elements gently surround Jerry's neuroception with cues of safety. The message to his unconscious mind—his body—is clear: "You are safe here with me."

Once Jerry senses enough safety cues, his body naturally shifts into an 'approach and connect' mode. This involuntary transition unlocks his social engagement behaviours, allowing him to fully participate in the coaching session.

I introduce Jerry to a series of simple, progressive exercises. Each builds on the last, giving him the agency to recognise and manage his 'patterns of protection' and transition into 'patterns of connection.' These exercises equip him with practical techniques for self-regulation, even in challenging situations.

Throughout this session, you'll witness the power of a well-paced NLP coaching dynamic. The coaching carefully balances compassion, humour, and challenge, maintaining steady momentum and progress. As NLP expert Michael Breen of MBNLP describes, effective coaching is about "pushing without being pushy." Notice that I don't provide Jerry with solutions. Instead, I support him in thinking and feeling differently, helping him rediscover his personal agency over his emotional state.

By the end of this chapter, you'll gain valuable insights into why establishing emotional safety is the foundation for meaningful coaching in the workplace. You'll also see how practical NLP techniques—rooted in neuro-resilience principles—can help team members overcome anxiety, navigate complex emotions, and build a resilient mindset that promotes long-term well-being.

To illustrate how these techniques extend beyond one-on-one coaching and into everyday leadership practices, let's turn to Steve, an in-house coach and trainer. Steve has been tasked with equipping leaders in his organisation with practical tools to support their teams during high-pressure situations. In the next section, you'll see how Steve uses the recorded session between Jerry and me as a teaching tool in a leadership development programme.

By breaking down the strategies and techniques used in Jerry's session, Steve guides leaders to understand how they can create emotionally safe environments for their own teams. This approach not only fosters trust and engagement but also empowers employees to manage stress effectively and build resilience in the face of workplace challenges.

As we step into the training room with Steve, reflect on how you might apply these insights to foster emotional safety and resilience within your own team. Let's observe how Steve bridges theory and practice, turning individual coaching insights into actionable leadership skills.

Coach Training Session

> *When the heart is agitated and angry,*
> *it is difficult for it to see clearly*
> **Zhuangzi**

Steve: "Good afternoon, everyone, and thank you for joining us today.

Before we begin, I want you to recall the *PACE Protocol*—a guiding structure designed to help you stay oriented throughout a neuro-resilience coaching session. Especially when working with individuals dealing with stress, trauma, or deeply rooted emotional challenges, coaches must heighten their awareness to remain fully attuned to the participant's verbal and non-verbal cues.

No two conversations are ever the same. Coaching sessions are fluid by nature and can drift in unexpected directions. This fluidity can make it easy to lose track of where the session is heading. The simplicity of the PACE structure keeps the coach grounded because each phase serves a distinct purpose. A helpful orienting question to ask yourself is:

"What goal am I pursuing now, and next?"

An early component of the *'Permission'* phase is what we call *safety priming*. Now, while this term is often mentioned, let's unpack its true significance. As coaches, leaders, or facilitators, we know that no meaningful progress can be made unless our clients feel genuinely safe. This sense of safety extends far beyond physical comfort—it's about generating enough cues of safety that the participant's neuroception shifts into a more connected and open state. As this connection deepens, the client naturally gives us permission to challenge them and help them make meaningful changes.

Safety priming involves subtle but deliberate verbal and non-verbal cues that signal to the participant that it is safe to approach, engage, and connect. As we receive signals of readiness, we continue to gently press and test for permission to guide the session forward.

In today's session, you'll observe Paul O'Neill, founder of *Neuro-Elevation Skills*, working within the *PACE Protocol* framework, applying a range of strategies and techniques to help the participant move naturally from one phase to the next. This willingness to transition to the next phase is a key indicator of the participant granting permission.

As you watch, pay close attention to how Paul engages with Jerry to address the lingering effects of workplace trauma—not through one-size-fits-all solutions but through a deliberate, structured process. This approach allows Jerry's instinctive responses to settle into emotional safety while his cognitive awareness begins to reaffirm his personal agency.

Notice how Paul transmits cues of safety using attentive listening, reframing, voice tone, and humour to prime Jerry's nervous system for deeper engagement. This intentional strategy helps Jerry gradually shift from anxiety and disconnection to a grounded state of calm and control.

This session underscores the importance of amplifying safety throughout the priming process. Paul's gentle questioning and subtle interventions steadily strengthen Jerry's sense of control over his emotions. By the end of this initial phase, Jerry isn't just calmer—he's primed for deeper, more transformative work.

As you observe, focus on the delicate balance between pressing forward and easing back, the ebb and flow of guiding the session, and the nuanced art of *probing for permission*. By following this structure, you'll see how neuro-resilient coaching moves beyond surface-level fixes to create lasting, meaningful change.

As I play the video, notice that safety priming begins from the moment of first contact. I'll signal to you as we transition through the remaining three phases of the *PACE Protocol*".

Video Session

Paul: *"Nice to see you, Jerry. How can I help you today?"*

Jerry: *(Looking tense) "I've been going through a bit of a rough patch."*

Paul: *(Softly) "A rough patch. What makes it that way?"*

Jerry: *(Pauses, looking down) "It feels like I'm drowning. Work's just been... relentless. Every time I think I'm getting a handle on things, something else comes at me."*

Paul: *(Nods) "Drowning... just trying to keep your head above water?"*

Jerry: *(Breathes out sharply) "Exactly. It's like... just when I come up for air, something else pulls me under. It's exhausting."*

Paul: *"It sounds exhausting."*

Jerry: *(Nods) "Yeah... and I'm not sure how much longer I can keep doing this."*

Paul: *(Slight smile) "Drowning isn't something you can do forever, right?"*

Jerry: *(Faint smile, still tense) "No, it's not. I'm tired. I'm weary."*

Paul: *(Playfully) "Well, unless you decide to develop gills, we're going to have to figure something else out, eh?"*

Jerry: *(Chuckles softly) "No gills, I'm afraid."*

Paul: *(Leaning back, giving him space) "Alright, well, good to know. No gills, no superpowers. So, here's a question, how do you know when it's time to be pulled down exactly?"*

Jerry: *(Looks straight at Paul) "I don't know what you mean."*

Paul: *"Well, the drowning thing is a metaphor for how it feels, right?"*

Jerry: *"Right."*

Paul: (Nodding) *"So, what I'm asking is, 'How do you know that it's the right time to feel like you're being pulled down and drowning?'"*

Jerry: (Eyebrows furrowed) *"I'm not actually making that decision."*

Paul: (Nodding in agreement) *"Sure, not consciously, but something inside you is making that decision, isn't it? I mean, it's not your office desk or your computer, is it?"*

It's just like water always boils at the same temperature. At whatever height above sea level it is, water always knows when to start boiling. At sea level, it knows to boil at 100°C and at the top of Mount Everest, it always boils at 68°C.

It's the same with your body, once something happens in a certain situation, your body always knows that it is time to feel like it's drowning.

Jerry: (Looking incredulous) *"I'm not picking and choosing, Paul. I've got a condition!"*

Paul: (In complete agreement) *"Yes... exactly! That's my point: it's conditional. Your feelings of being pulled under is conditional on something happening on the outside, in some particular circumstances, that leads to you feeling like drowning. Yeah?"*

Jerry: (Nodding as though following along) *"OK"*

Paul: *"So, what I want to know is 1) what's the situation and 2) what's the thing that leads to the bad feeling? For example, do you get the bad feeling at home, at work, on holiday?"*

Jerry: *"Mostly at work. Sometimes at home."*

Paul: *"Right. Mostly at work and sometimes at home. Let's start at home. When does it usually happen?"*

Jerry: *"It depends on my shift pattern. I fly in and out of a mine site. Typically, it's building for two or three days before I take the flight back to work. But it really kicks in on the evening before."*

Paul: *"And this is the typical pattern?"*

Jerry: *"Yes."*

Paul: *"OK. So, it is conditional. Just like the water, you begin warming up for a couple of days before going back to work; and then you're at full boiling point the night before. Give yourself a crappy night's sleep. Then get yourself to work, both cranked up and tired. Ready for the fortnight ahead. Right?"*

Jerry: (Nodding. Looking down.) *"Pretty much."*

Paul: *"And, let me guess, you maintain this tension constantly just waiting for something to go wrong. And as nothing ever goes perfectly, something will always go wrong. And that's what pushes you over the edge. Or, rather, pulls you under and you feel like you're drowning."*

Jerry: (Nodding. Looking down.) *"Exactly."*

Paul: (In a reflective tone) *"Hmmm... well, that would do it. But have you ever thought of not doing this. I mean there has to be an easier way. I mean, how about you just feel nice and calm all the way through and then freak out only when something imperfect happens. That way at least you're calmer almost all of the time. Better still, why don't you stay pumped up and joyful all the time and, if something goes wrong, you put it right without any freaking out. Have you thought about doing it that way?"*

Jerry: (Frowning. Shaking his head) *"That would be great but it's not like I have that choice. It's like I'm locked into this tension and anxiety all the time"*.

Paul: (In an upbeat tone and demeanour) *"You're locked into these* bad feelings? I think we need to get you locked out from them. Don't you? Wouldn't that be better?"

Jerry: (Still looking unconvinced) "Of course".

Paul: (Inquisitively) "So, back to the two to three days before your about to fly into work. How do you know, two days out, it's time to make yourself feel bad."

Jerry: (Looking exasperated) "What?"

Paul: (Conversationally) "Well, my guess is that you start to make nasty pictures inside your mind of the kind of crappy imperfection that could lead to you feeling pulled under. That's my guess but it's your brain. So, what happens?"

Jerry: (Looking pensive) "Yes. I run scenarios that I am likely to be facing when I get back on site."

Paul: (Eyebrows up and smiling) "Happy scenarios where you are like a superhero, things go wrong, and you swoop in and put them right? Or maybe it's something a bit more horrible?"

Jerry: (Looking pensive) "I think about the things that could go wrong. The kind of things that would make me look bad."

Paul: (Sardonically) "Ah, yes. Just to get you in the mood! And to whom are you going to be looking bad?"

Jerry: (Slight smile) "The boss. I'm a bit intimidated by him."

Paul: (Inquisitively) "A bit? You're a lot intimidated by him! But why? Is he a gangster or tyrant or something? Is he likely to have you publicly flogged? What do you imagine is going to happen, exactly?"

Jerry: (Smiling a little. Eyes looking up. Pauses.) "I don't really know. I jolt myself out of the thought before I get to that part. I just picture his eyes, and I'm snapped out of it."

Paul: (In mock amazement) "But you're missing the best part – the finale! At least if you watch a scary movie all the way to the end, you at least get to the end... and then it's over! What you're doing is pausing the movie right at the cliffhanger, it's never over. You start the whole crappy thing again, all the way up to the cliffhanger and stop it again. It's like a loop that runs and runs and you never get to the end and see the final credits! You've really learned to stress yourself out like a pro. When are you flying back on site?"

Jerry: (Looks bemused.) "Three days."

Paul: (Enthused) So, the bad feeling is pretty much due! Cool. Well, that makes things a lot easier. What I want you to do is stop, backup and... [Paul blinks] close your eyes.

Jerry: (Closes his eyes)

[Video pauses]

Steve: Notice that Jerry complied immediately with the request to close his eyes. This is evidence that he had given Paul permission to progress.

Paul moves to the new goal of proving to Jerry that he has personal agency and control over his emotions.

[Video resumes]

Paul: (Vocal prosody) "That's right. Just go deep inside and begin to imagine all the scenarios that you know you are about to run through now. See what you will see. Hear what you will hear and begin to bring back all that anxiety. Have you got it?"

Jerry: (Slight nod)

Paul: "I want you to make the picture vivid and bright, sharp and clear. Can you hear sounds?"

Jerry: (Slight nod) "Yes."

Paul: "OK. Make those sounds crisper and richer. And really feel that feeling strongly now. Have you got that?"

Jerry: (Flat expression. Looking Paler) "Yes."

Paul: (Gentle tones. Downward vocal commands) "Ok. Where is the bad feeling in your body? Show me. Touch it with your hand."

Jerry: (Touches his upper chest)

Paul: (Prosodic tones) "Now, the feeling needs to keep moving to keep the feeling going. Still using your hand, show me where it moves to."

Jerry: (Pauses. Moves his hand to his stomach): "It moves here."

Paul: (Prosodic tones) "Excellent. Now the feeling isn't just going to sit there. It still has to move to sustain itself. Typically, it will move in a circle. It could feel like its rolling inside of you. Show me the direction and speed with your hand now. That's right, just like that."

Jerry: (Begins to move his hand clockwise over his stomach): "It's going this way."

Paul: (Prosodic tones) "Now. I'm going to get you to do a couple of things. At first, it will feel a bit worse, but it will come to a fun conclusion. Alright, now, give me a colour for this feeling."

Jerry: "Black."

Paul: "Spin the black feeling faster. I want an honest, complete doubling of the black feeling. You can keep using your hand if that helps. Let me know when you're there."

Jerry: (hand moving faster) "I'm there."

Paul: "Are you feeling better or worse?"

Jerry: "Worse."

Paul: (*Enthusiastic tones*) *"Perfect! Now bring it back down to its original speed... are you there?"*

Jerry: (*Slows his hand down. Nods*).

Paul: *"Now, down to 50%. Let me know."*

Jerry: (*Hand slows further. Slight nod*).

Paul: *"Now, 25%.... and stop it dead... now begin to reverse it... take it to 50% speed."*

Jerry: (*Hand begins to move anticlockwise*).

[*Video pauses*]

Steve: Jerry has demonstrated that he can dial up and down his negative emotion. This is personal agency and control. This is a strong counter example to Jerry's earlier assertion, when he said, "I'm not actually making that decision".

With these criteria satisfied, Paul now begins to assist Jerry into generating positive feelings.

[*Video resumes*]

Paul: *"Give me a new colour"*

Jerry: (*Shoulders relaxing*) *"Bright yellow"*

Paul: *"Now double the good feeling. A complete, honest full doubling"*

Jerry: (*Continuing to relax. Breathing Abdominally. Slight nod.*)

Paul: *"Now keep this good feeling spinning and look at the scenarios that used to scare you. How do you feel about them now"*

Jerry: (*Colour returning to his face*) *"I feel better."*

Paul: *"Out of ten, where one is the crappy feeling and ten is the most relaxed and carefree you've ever been, where are you?"*

Jerry: *"I'm at five."*

Paul: (Prosodic voice) *"Wonderful. For the rest of the session, the most important thing that I want you to do is to keep this good feeling spinning. Round and round and round. If you are visualising it on the outside, pull the yellow feeling in, so the full relaxing intensity is inside your body. That's right – just like that."*

Jerry: (Rolls his head up. Mouth opening slightly).

Paul: (Prosodic voice) *"Now spin this feeling up to the top of your head. Down to the tips of your toes. Let this lovely yellow feeling just wash all over you. Bathe every cell in your skin, ever sinew of muscle, every synapse in your brain with this feeling of deep, deeper, deepest relaxation.*

And, as you do so, just let your mind begin to sense your whole body go flippy and floppy. And I want you to think back to a time when you felt truly calm and serene. Maybe it was a time when you were on a peaceful holiday, or perhaps just a quiet moment at home where everything felt just right. Can you bring that to mind?"

Jerry: (Pauses, a small smile creeping onto his face) "Yeah... I'm thinking of a time at the beach. Just sitting by the water, listening to the waves."

Paul: "Perfect. Now I want you to step back into that memory. See what you saw, hear what you heard, and most importantly, feel what you felt. Let yourself be there, at the beach, completely calm and safe."

(Jerry's shoulders visibly relax even more, his breathing slow and steady.)

Paul: (Rhythmic and prosodic vocal patterns) "As you feel that calm... calmer... calmer... calmest still. I want you to pour and spin it into *your good feeling. Let it sparkle and let it shine. Let bliss spread inside your mind. Imagine it growing, spreading through your body. Feel the relaxation softening your body. Soft... softer... softest... ever so gently, ever so softly. How does that feel?"*

Jerry: *"It feels... good... Really peaceful."*

[*Video pauses*]

Steve: "Really peaceful" is a wonderful place to have assisted a traumatised colleague or client. It is as far away from trauma as a frog is from feathers. In doing so, the third criteria-set as been met.

Paul is now able to continue to the fourth goal: integrating new learnings and establishing new skills. We call these 'autoregulation strategies'.

[*Video resumes*]

Paul: *"Good. Now, I want you to keep that feeling with you by building a button that is a better button, probably the best button of your life. By pressing your thumb and middle finger together, gently.*

Now, some people wonder whether the button is on the finger, being pressed by the thumb. Others think that it's on the thumb and is being pressed by the finger. But the truth is there's a button on both your thumb and your finger. And because you've got two buttons on you, it's going to work doubly well for you.

From this day on and for the rest of your life, you are going to be able to become more relaxed than you've ever been now."

(*Jerry presses his thumb and middle finger together, and you can see his body fully relax.*)

Paul: *"Keep spinning the good feeling and say, just at the back of your* *mind, the lovely word 'soften' and feel your whole body deepen its relaxation, bliss and peacefulness."*

(Jerry's face shows visible relaxation, a soft smile on his lips.)

Paul: "Now, I want you to imagine it's the morning that you're heading back to work. Picture yourself waking up. Maybe you're still in bed, maybe you're brushing your teeth—whatever part of your morning routine you want to imagine. But this time, you're carrying that sense of deep relaxation with you. How do you see yourself starting the day?"

Jerry: *(Pauses, closing his eyes)* "I see myself... calm. I've slept well. I'm not rushing around like I usually do. I'm just... taking my time."

Paul: "Great. Now, keep the good feeling spinning inside of you. And once you double it, press your thumb and middle finger together. How does it feel to start your day like this?"

Jerry: *(Smiling slightly)* "It feels... easy. Like I'm in control."

Paul: "Perfect. Now, let's move forward a bit. You're stepping off the flight and walking onto site. Picture yourself walking in, your usual route, seeing your colleagues, getting to your office, seeing your desk. How does that feel?"

Jerry: *(Nods)* "It feels good. I'm walking in like... I'm not worried about anything. I know I can handle whatever comes my way."

Paul: "That's exactly what we want. Now, imagine you've got a challenge waiting for you—a difficult meeting or a tight deadline. But this time, your body is ready, and your mind is prepared. You're feeling calm, confident, and wrapped in a deep sense of wellbeing. See yourself going into that situation. How does it play out?"

Jerry: *(Pauses, his expression softening)* "It's different. I'm not tense. I'm listening more, and I'm speaking up when I need to. I'm not second-guessing myself."

Paul: "Wonderful. And when the meeting's over, how do you feel?"

Jerry: "Relieved. But not just relieved—happy, like I handled it, and I'm proud of how I did."

Paul: (Smiling warmly) "That's it! That's what this is all about. Open your eyes and keep the good feeling spinning. How are you feeling?"

Jerry: (Smiling) "I'm still calm. I'm just so relaxed."

Paul: "Exactly. You've turned your anxiety around."

Jerry: "It's amazing how different I feel. I never thought I could change how I felt like this."

Paul: "Out of ten, how does this new sense of calm feel compare to where you were at the beginning of our session?"

Jerry: (Pausing, smiling) "It's a ten. It feels... lighter. Like a weight's been lifted. I feel like... I can handle whatever comes my way now."

Paul: "And isn't that exactly what we were aiming for? You've done incredibly well, Jerry, and I want you to remember this sense of calm, and keep spinning the good feeling because, the truth is, you have always held inside you the capacity to feel good despite all the challenges, you just needed to be shown how to tap into it. Now you know that control is always within you. Anytime you need it, just spin that good feeling and press your thumb and finger together. It's all yours."

Jerry: (Nods, smiling) "Thank you, Paul. This has been... life-changing."

Paul: "You did all the hard work, Jerry. Now, just keep practicing for the rest of the session, and you'll find that this calm becomes second nature. And because you're in control of how your body can feel now, we can move on and do something that will help you over the coming days."

[Video paused]

Coach's Wrap-Up

Steve: "OK. I'll pause it there. What we've just seen is a very fluent application of the *PACE Protocol* in real-time. Each phase naturally flows on the last. This structure ensures that the participant is shifted from stress to calm to optimism. There's no need to rush, the PACE Protocol allows you to immerse yourself in the moment, without losing track. Just focus on doing each of the thousand little jobs well.

So, when you're in your next session, ask yourself:

'Which phase of PACE am I in now, and what's the next goal criteria?'

As leaders, our role isn't to eliminate pressure – that's impossible. Rather it is to equip our people with tools that prevent negative stressors from disconnecting and overwhelming them. It's to give them the ability to manage their stressors beyond this session: *safe from the skin in.*

This is the essence of neuro-resilience coaching: helping people feel safe from the inside out. It is *personal enhancement* to provide them the tools to make permanent changes.

Let's open the floor for any questions."

Q&A Session

Question 1: "*How do you know when someone is ready to move on from safety priming to something else?*"

Steve: "*Nice question. It really comes down to paying attention to the client's responses, both their verbal and non-verbal. When Jerry started to smile more, laugh a little, and his body was becoming more relaxed, and his breathing was becoming more abdominal. Whilst not definitive, they were indicative that Jerry's body was feeling safe enough to move forward.*

These indicators don't have to be unambiguous "green-to-go" signals: just get them from red to amber, then prime for safety and probe for permission. There's no need to rush, just be alert for the cues in: even if the door's ajar, it's open, so step right in.

Paul also used humour to press and test for permission—we call this 'probing'—if the client smiles or laughs or sees the funny side of their own predicament, even in part or somewhat, it's a cue they're body is ready to move on. It's about building safety and trust incrementally, but consistently; and testing gently, and taking the safety cues from the client."

QUESTION 2: "HOW DOES THE 'SPINNING' *technique actually work to reduce anxiety?"*

Steve: *"This is a terrific technique. It's another great example of changing someone's subjective reality, changes their objective reality. Spinning is a way of tapping into the body's natural kinaesthetic responses to emotions. Anxiety has a particular movement—a particular direction and speed.*

But everyone is slightly different, which means you've got to take the time to uncover it. Sometimes the process is quicker with some people than others. By tracking and tracing this movement and then deliberately changing its speed – faster and slower – the person begins to understand that they have agency over that unpleasant emotion: they can make it more intense, then less intense.

When they reverse the direction of the spin, they change the feeling to something else. They begin to gain control over multiple feelings. It's a terrific piece of submodality work, where the sensory qualities of an experience are altered to change how we feel about it. As such, by learning to manipulate their own subjective experience, they are learning to change their metabolism. Their biology."

. . .

QUESTION 3: *"What if the person doesn't have a strong memory of feeling calm, for the 'Wrapped in Serenity' technique?"*

Steve: *"That's actually more common than you might think, especially with people dealing with trauma or long-term stress. However, most people get tired and exhausted enough to fall asleep. You can tap into that feeling and amplify it.*

Even then, if a specific memory doesn't come to mind, we can use hypnosis and guided meditation to create an experience of calm. Then amplify that. The key is to make it really relaxing by using the individual's particular submodalities across all the senses to imagine the colours, sounds, and sensations of a peaceful scene.

Don't make the mistake that visual submodalities always need to be bright and vivid. Sometimes a person will associate better with more subdued submodalities. It is important to pace them. By helping people to uncover the visual and auditory qualities that works best for them, the more effective coaching will be. It's about giving each individual an experience of calm, even if it's one they're creating for the first time."

QUESTION 4: *"How does future pacing help solidify the change?"*

Steve: *"Future pacing is about getting people to imagine themselves successfully practicing their new exercises in real-life situations. In Jerry's case, Paul asked him to visualise himself at work the next day, handling stress with calm and control. By doing this, Jerry starts to associate the calm feeling with future events.*

This not only weakens or collapses the old anchors at his place of work, but it's also more likely that Jerry will actually use the techniques when the things that used to trigger him pop up. It's a way of mentally rehearsing success, making the new behaviours feel more natural and automatic when the time comes.

. . .

WELL, it looks like we've covered everything for now. I hope this session has given you valuable insights into safety priming in neuro-resilience coaching and how to support people who are navigating a disconnected state.

Remember, the key isn't to rush in with solutions but to build trust and create emotional safety at a pace that each individual can handle. Everyone is different, so continue to push gently, probe thoughtfully, and always test for permission. Once that foundation is solid, the rest becomes so much easier.

But the most important takeaway today is this: people aren't broken—they're simply running protective strategies that no longer serve them. Our role as leaders and coaches isn't to fix them but to offer better choices—choices that empower them to build stronger, more resilient versions of themselves.

So, take what you've learned today and begin integrating these tools into your leadership approach. Every moment you invest in creating safety and trust is a step toward a more resilient, engaged, and high-performing team.

Thank you all for your participation and questions!"

NINE
RUPTURE PREVENTION

We are what we repeatedly do.
Excellence, then, is not an act, but a habit
Aristotle

HOW TO REPAIR SAFETY RUPTURES, after they've occurred, was explored in Chapter Eight. This chapter shifts focus to prevention. After all, what's better than recovery? Never needing it in the first place. By integrating simple yet effective practices into daily routines, leaders can fortify themselves against the pressures that trigger breakdowns like Jerry's, safeguarding not only their well-being but also that of their teams and organisations.

In this chapter, we will explore the importance of daily autoregulation routines, along with ad hoc practices for managing moments when things don't go as planned. As Benjamin Franklin wisely said,

---

"An ounce of prevention is worth a pound of cure"

With that advice in mind, let's examine the practices that have helped many people I've worked with over the years—bearing in mind two important caveats:

1. **Everyone is Different.** Different techniques work better for different people. Most individuals discover that it's not a single practice but a particular combination of routines that best supports their well-being. Part of your journey is to experiment and identify what works best for your unique needs.
2. **Consistency is Key.** Once you find the techniques that truly work for you—keep doing them! You might be surprised how often people abandon their routines once they start feeling good, only to find themselves stressed again. The smarter approach is to commit to your bespoke autoregulation routine for life, refining it as needed. After all, perfection isn't some vague ideal; it's the disciplined practice of doing many small things exceptionally well. In the world of NLP, this means continuously fine-tuning and adjusting your sensory submodalities to optimise your state.

Preventing emotional ruptures begins with mastering your own internal state. One of the most effective ways to build this internal resilience is by integrating the PACE Protocol—not just as a tool for recovery, but as a proactive daily practice. Let's explore how PACE can become the foundation of your emotional resilience.

PACE Yourself

The PACE Protocol isn't just a tool for repairing safety ruptures—it's even more powerful in preventing them. When you make PACE part of your daily life, you don't just recover from stress—you create a mindset where stress struggles to take hold in the first place. Its strength lies in building emotional resilience and safeguarding your emotional safety and, by extension, your psychological safety. Before you can effectively lead others, you must first command your own internal state. Leadership begins within.

When you weave the four phases of the PACE Protocol into your daily life, you create an unshakable foundation. This isn't about scrambling to recover after stress strikes; it's about building a mental and emotional terrain where stress can't take root. Resilience isn't a reaction—it's a proactive stance. Let's explore how each step of the PACE Protocol fortifies your personal resilience.

Permission is the gateway to intentional leadership. Too often, we drift into our day, half-engaged and mentally unprepared. Granting yourself permission isn't passive—it's a deliberate choice to step forward with purpose and confidence. It's about silencing self-doubt and reclaiming your authority over the day ahead. Before diving into your tasks, ask yourself:

> *"Have I given myself full permission today to lead with presence and confidence?"*

This small but powerful check-in transforms you from a bystander in your own life to an active, intentional leader.

Whilst you can't control everything when 'shit happens' but you can choose how you respond. Instinct wants you to react. Resilience gives you response choices. This is where cognitive *Agency* over instinctual patterns comes in. Pausing to notice whether your actions stem from instinct or thoughtful choice gives you back control. Consider this question before acting:

> *"How much of my next action is driven by instinct and how much by cognition?"*

This moment of reflection interrupts automatic reactions and opens the door for better decisions.

Connection is where leadership truly breathes because leadership is a social activity. Leading isn't about control—it's about connection. It's about meeting people where they are, having tough conversations, celebrating wins, and challenging your team to grow. But you can't engage others if you're stuck in a disconnected survival mode. Leadership flourishes when you're grounded, calm, and open. Pause and ask yourself:

> *"Do I have full access to my social engagement behaviours?"*

If the answer is no, it's time to reset. Your ability to inspire others depends on your ability to connect.

Finally, *Embedding* the new functional strategies, meanings and frames. Resilience isn't a one-off effort—it must be embedded into how you operate. This is about turning resilience into habit, so it becomes as natural as breathing. Mental rehearsal is key here. Elite athletes don't wait for the game to start practicing—they prepare mentally and physically. Leaders must do the same. Ask yourself:

> *"Which situations can I pre-live or pre-frame to handle better?"*

By visualising and planning ahead, you train your mind to navigate challenges with agility.

PACE Yourself is about consistent, conscious engagement with how you lead yourself. Neuro-resilience is built primarily through simple, consistent habits. So, let's turn our focus to practical daily routines that can seamlessly support you—starting and ending your day on the right note.

. . .

Bliss List

When was the last time you felt completely at ease, filled with joy and energy? Stressors are all around us. They are constantly attempting to pulls us towards stress and negativity. Reclaiming those moments can transform your resilience. A powerful way to cultivate positive emotional states is through a *Bliss List*—a personalised collection of joyful memories and sensory experiences that spark calm, energy, and vitality. Our brains naturally gravitate toward negative experiences, a survival instinct that once protected us but can overwhelm us in today's world. The Bliss List serves as a strategic countermeasure, guiding your mind to amplify positivity and build lasting emotional resilience.

Crafting a Bliss List is more than recalling random happy moments—it's about intentionally selecting diverse experiences that evoke different kinds of positivity: excitement, serenity, satisfaction, and connection. Include significant milestones, like achieving a career goal, alongside small, everyday pleasures, such as feeling the warmth of sunlight on your face. Balance active joys, like dancing or hiking, with passive comforts, like listening to soothing music or sipping a quiet cup of tea.

To deepen its impact, fully engage all five senses. When revisiting these moments, make the colours more vibrant, the sounds richer, and the sensations more vivid. Imagine the steady rhythm of your footsteps on a forest path, the cool air brushing your skin, or the sound of laughter echoing with friends. This sensory richness intensifies the emotional effect, priming your nervous system for calm and confidence.

Tailor your Bliss List to fit your emotional needs. On sluggish mornings, revisit energising memories—a thrilling adventure, a hard-won success, or spontaneous laughter. When anxiety creeps in, focus on grounding experiences like the steady rhythm of your footsteps on a forest path or quiet moments of reflection. In moments of self-doubt, recall achievements that reaffirm your competence and strength.

Building and maintaining your Bliss List is an evolving practice. Reflect regularly on past joys, imagine future delights, and enrich your memories with sensory detail. Over time, this simple yet profound tool becomes a reliable resource for emotional balance, helping you navigate daily stressors with strength and composure.

Start now. Write down three moments that light you up inside. This is more than a list—it's your foundation for resilience, calm, and boundless energy.

For example, Sarah, a marketing executive, starts her day by revisiting the memory of hiking a mountain trail, feeling the cool breeze and hearing the crunch of leaves underfoot. This simple act energises her for the challenges ahead.

Research in positive psychology shows that intentionally recalling joyful experiences can rewire the brain for resilience and well-being (Fredrickson, 2001). Let your Bliss List be your guide to harnessing that power.

Easy Daily Practices

For most of my clients and trainees, just a ten-minute morning and/or nighttime routine is enough to make a significant difference. If the first thing you do upon waking is to feel safe, energised, and connected, you're off to a great start. Similarly, if the last thing you do before drifting into sleep is to feel calm, safe, and grounded, you're far more likely to enjoy restful and restorative sleep.

Even with solid routines in place, life's unexpected disruptions can throw you off balance. To stay resilient, it's essential to clear emotional clutter before it builds up. This next section introduces powerful techniques to release lingering stress and prevent small setbacks from becoming major disruptions.

Bosses, spouses, kids, colleagues, and clients are abundant sources of disruption to even the most contented mind. Beyond interpersonal triggers, the world itself offers its share of challenges: bad weather, traffic delays, minor illnesses, and, more seriously, life-altering events like job loss, breakups, or bereavement.

We'll address how to navigate significant disruptions shortly. But first, let's focus on foundational morning and nighttime routines designed to strengthen your emotional resilience and keep you centred—regardless of what the day brings.

"Rise & Shine" Patterns

To create an effective *Rise & Shine* routine, start by identifying activities that make you feel truly energised. This can be done by making a short 'Bliss List' of sensory-rich experiences—things you are naturally drawn to when you see, hear, touch, smell, or taste them. These should be moments or ideas that evoke positive energy and motivation.

If You Wake Up Groggy...

If you, like me, are a bit groggy in the morning, make sure what you put on that list are the kinds of things that get you bouncing out of bed in the morning. Before I knew that there were more pleasant alternatives, I used to motivate myself out of bed by hearing my father's booming (slightly threatening) voice, yelling,

---

"Move!"

The jolt of adrenaline worked a treat in getting me up, out and to the gym. But I've found more pleasant ways that work even better.

One of the simplest and most effective techniques is breath control. Starting with box breathing—inhaling for four counts, holding for four, and exhaling for four—helps balance oxygen flow and energises the body. This breathing method activates the parasympathetic nervous system, which helps regulate energy levels and prepare the body for action. After three or so rounds, turn your focus to your Bliss List.

Recall energising experiences: socialising with great friends, laughing at something really funny, making love with energy and passion, or cheering for your favourite sports team as they win the championship, engaging in a competitive activity like skiing, debating or riding a roller-coaster.

Whatever gets you thrilled, get it on your list and get into your morning: replay it in your mind vividly... relive it convincingly, just like the song, *"Right here! Right now!"*.

See what you saw and hear what you heard. Make the colours brighter and the images bigger. Make the sounds crisper, richer and louder. Begin to feel the energy running through your whole body. And begin to grin as the thrill builds. Then, at the back of your mind, with a voice like rolling thunder, say:

"This day is <u>mine</u>!"

If You Wake Up Anxious...

On the other hand, if you are apt to wake up in the morning feeling slightly apprehensive or, perhaps, worrying about the day; that's OK, it's only your body has shifted into a 'pattern of protection'. Just take this as a sign that your body is running this strategy because it needs to begin to *feel safe and connected.*

Again, breathing is an easy first step, so you might begin with some *4-7-8 breathing*—inhale for four counts, hold for seven, and exhale for eight. This breathing technique helps slow the heart rate and engages the vagus nerve, calming the nervous system and reducing anxiety.

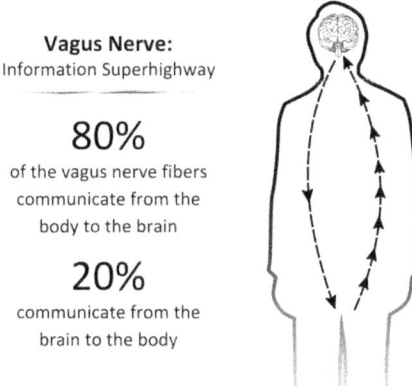

Vagus Nerve:
Information Superhighway

80%
of the vagus nerve fibers communicate from the body to the brain

20%
communicate from the brain to the body

ONCE YOU BEGIN to feel calmer, think about activities where you feel competent and at ease. This maybe a hobby, such as golf or badminton or playing poker. It could be a skill in which you have achieved excellence over the years, such as woodwork or painting or cooking. Or it may be something that, soon after beginning the activity, you go into a heightened state of focus, such as dancing, running, playing an instrument, gardening, walking in nature or writing.

Whatever it is that gives you that grounded feeling of certainty, replay it in your mind. Again, do it as though you are reliving it "right here, right now". See what you saw and hear what you heard. Make the colours brighter and bolder. Then push the images away from you and, as you do so, make them grow bigger; so they become as large as a giant *Imax* screen.

Make the sounds crisp, clear and resonant. Begin to feel a deep sense of grounded surety running through every vein and oozing from every pore. Feel that sense of *'in the moment'* focus and calm resolve spreading through your whole body. And, at the back of your mind with a deep sense of absolute truth, say:

"Today… belongs… to me!"

The Power of Conviction

Remember, the purpose of doing these practices is to prime your body with the right metabolic state for a terrific day ahead. Therefore, it's got to be convincing! If you say, *"today belongs to me"* in a weak, wimpy, wishy-washy, zero-conviction voice... you're not going change your state!

However, if you are fully committed, and say it and hear it with the rich, rhythmic and resonant voice of Morgan Freeman, you will feel more calm, more grounded and more confident.

Own it. Let this powerful start carry you through your day.

Get Rid of It

Things can trigger us because we are alive, and our body wants to keep it that way. In doing so, we can get angry to the point of seething; scared to the point of being petrified; saddened to the point of total deflation. With a close associate, I refer to this phenomenon as, the *Wobble*. Every two to three months, she experiences a mini 'Jerry Moment'. Like the straws on the proverbial camel's back, things build up... then the back breaks.

Of course, it is not the sheer quantity of unpleasant experiences she has amassed between wobbles that causes the next wobble. Rather, like all of us, her brain is compelled to revisit these unfortunate moments again and again. Yet, each revisiting is itself a bad experience; therefore, she generates the majority of the straws herself until... 'Wobble'!

This going back and picking through bad times is known as *rumination*, which is another pattern of protection. Interestingly, like cows and sheep, camels also ruminate as they chew their cud (fun fact: camels are *pseudoruminants*). Our bodies revisit snippets of snarky comments, hushed tones, ambiguous gestures, fleeting glances or a verbal faux pas. They seek to yield some protective insight to what is going on, *right here, right now.*

"The threats and dangers of the future are hidden inside our prior bad experiences"

That is a basic program within our survival instinct, and it's gotten our species to where we are today. As a consequence, our bodies are constantly raking and sifting through the worse of our history. A relentless search for parallels and patterns to solve the problem of evading life-threatening moments in the future.

The price of this life-extending program is to diminish the quality of the very life the program has extended. Put simply, revisiting a bad memory in the brain means vividly reliving it in the body. Because each time we recall these bad memories, our adrenaline and cortisol levels begin to climb. We become fearful, angry and depressed. We become disconnected from others. But disconnected leader is no leader at all. A tyrant, a distraction or a burden, but not a leader.

Leaders face constant challenges—some predictable, others entirely unexpected. Without regular mental and emotional upkeep, these stressors can quietly accumulate. Much like physical hygiene, leaders must develop 'mental hygiene' practices to stay emotionally clear and effective:

- If you are in a leadership role where lots of things can and do go wrong, there's a lot of opportunity to become triggered.
- If you are in an executive role where there is a lot of ambiguity, uncertainty and complexity, you will be subject to shocks and surprises.

- If you're working in an aggressively competitive, unforgiving or toxic environment, where your integrity, intelligence and credibility can be called into question with scant evidential grounds, you will be subject to unfair criticism and cheap shots.

In all of these scenarios, you will fare better if you are able to sustain a calm, confident and connected state. If not, your likelihood of having a 'Jerry moment' is high and rising.

Leadership Hygiene Practice

Think of it like washing your dishes after a meal. The alternative? Eating off the same dirty plate again and again. Or consider taking the rubbish out when the kitchen bin is full. The alternative is letting waste pile up and rot in your home. Gross, right?

Yet many leaders don't "clean their neurology" after a stressful day or week. Like Jerry, they let disconnecting moments of disappointment, frustration, regret, embarrassment, fright and upset pile up. Then they go to bed and relive them all again. They fail to understand that *disconnection* is the denial of the body to heal itself – because human connection is the biological imperative to emotional safety and health. They forget two scientific truths:

1. *Disconnection* suppresses the body's natural ability to heal itself
2. *Connection* is a biological imperative for emotional safety and health.

So, let's wash away the mental clutter.

Bring to your mind a memory of a bad experience on which you have been ruminating. Start to adjust and noodle with the submodalities. Pause the movie and flicker it black and white quickly for a count of five. Then push the picture away from you so that it becomes tiny.

Repeat this five times quickly. Then go to the end of the memory and begin to rewind it so that people talk backwards and walk backwards. Play the memory backwards all the way to the beginning of the memory, so it stops just before the bad experience happened.

Begin to spin the same green feeling that you created in *Turning Anxiety Around* from Chapter 6 and rewind the movie faster. Do these three more times rewinding the memory faster and faster each time. As mentioned earlier, practice makes perfect and perfection is just about doing a lot of tiny things well. So, keep practicing this at the end of each difficult day.

This combination of techniques created by Richard Bandler has been widely used to help individuals manage negative emotions. In my view, they are a true gift to humanity. The formula is easy to remember:

- Flicker the picture black and white for a five-count.
- Shrink the picture, five times fast.
- Then play the sights, sounds and sensations backwards, five times fast.
- Done!

Get to Sleep

When it comes to getting to sleep, your body needs to feel safe and calm. However, people go to bed stressing about something silly or embarrassing or upsetting that happened during the day. Hopefully, we've taken care of that problem above. Make sure you practice the '*Get Rid of It*' exercise as soon as you practically can – there's no reason to hold onto a bad experience.

Once you've cleared the day's emotional clutter, the next step is ensuring a restful night's sleep. Sleep is your body's most powerful tool for restoration, but it's often compromised by unresolved stress. People go to bed worrying about and fretting over a meeting or encounter or some event that is going to happen the following day. They run and loop convincing disaster scenarios, thereby ensuring their adrenaline and cortisol levels are elevated right before bedtime.

Inevitably, they lie in bed 'determined' to get to sleep but, all the time, they are stressing about their upsetting hallucination. Convinced by their brain's scary scenario-playing, their body pumps more and more adrenaline into their system to mobilise them out of their bed and away from the imagined danger. Even more 'determined' to get to sleep, they roll over, punch their pillow, yank their covers back over themselves and go back to dwelling on and mulling over their scary thoughts.

Of course, this lack of fleeing from what their body interprets as "clear and present danger" induces it to pump even more adrenalin into their system. And so, this battle continues with the person's cognition simultaneously keeping themselves in a vulnerable position in bed as well as generating scary thoughts to which their body responds with increased escalation. With practice, their body learns that going to bed is very unsafe and perfects its stress response every night.

I ask such people what they would think if I recommended that they drink a couple of cans of Red Bull before going to bed. They always say that would be a stupid thing to do because it would keep them awake. And I am forced to agree with them. Then I say,

"But at least the Red Bull won't scare you. So, what is more stupid, taking the Red Bull or scaring yourself every night into persistent or chronic insomnia?"

Of course, they claim that they don't have a choice, that it is out of their control and that it just keeps happening. This is all complete nonsense, of course, but they are convinced of it. So, for all the people out there that either can't get to sleep or, if they wake up in the middle of the night, can't get back to sleep, let's explore how to transition smoothly into deep, restorative rest.

The first of which is to have a short mental list of things that, when you did them, you felt deep satisfaction and gentle joy. As a clue, bungy-jumping, rollercoasters and theme parks are not what I have in mind. I'm thinking more along the lines of listening to soothing music, getting a gentle massage, lazing in the sun, a cool glass of water on a hot day, children giggling, slowly completing a jigsaw puzzle, feeling satiated after a big meal, a beautiful smile.

Whatever should be on your *'Bliss List'*, write it down. Look at the completed list itself. Make a picture of it in your mind. Check that you have commit it to memory by recalling the remembered picture of the list. Test yourself by reading each line in your mind with a soft and sleepy inner voice. This is important because, as I joke with my clients, the word 'relax' is called <u>re</u>-lax because you have to do it several times. Otherwise, it would just have been called... 'lax'!

So, we are going to begin to relax several times in several ways. And, once more, begin with your breath. Just notice from where it is you are breathing – is it high in the chest or low in the abdomen? If it is high in the chest, begin to move it lower with every passing breath. As you do so, begin to breathe slower. When you breathe in, notice how much your lungs inflate. Calibrate to this level and, when you breathe out, count to two before breathing in to the same level. Breathe out, hold for two, and breathe in. Repeat and on the third intake of breath, *take twice as long to fill your lungs half as much.*

Now, use the *Connect with Yourself* technique and turn on your 'light of joy', which is just one inch below your bellybutton. Feel the light moving as you breathe in and out, and how it stays still for a count of two after you have exhaled. Picture your *Bliss List* and read the first line in that soft and sleepy voice and then relive that peaceful relaxing moment in your life. Let your body go all flippy and floppy, so that every patch of your skin, every fold and every follicle just softens completely. Keep the 'count for two' breath pattern going and, at each count of two, let a gentle wave of relaxation bathe every cell, every sinew and every synapse in *softened bliss*.

Keeping your mind reliving the first item on your list and, even as you do, allow yourself to go to other lovely, related times. If your brain goes to something less pleasant, that's OK, it just means that it's time to go to the second item on your list. And, as you do, turn up your joy light and let it begin to spread through your whole body. Picture your list and read the next line in that soft sleepy voice and fall into the memory completely. Relive the sumptuous sights, sounds and sensations just as you lived them. Feel your body soften completely and, during the count of two, feel a wave of bliss and peacefulness wash over your body.

Sometimes you can wake up in the middle of the night; perhaps from a 'call of nature' or from an upset child. When you get back to bed, settle down and get comfortable. Then, ever so slowly, softly and gently, just curl your toes up a little bit and let a sleepy smile move through your body. Let it come up to your mouth, up and into your mind. Turn your joy light on and return to the next line on the Bliss List. Remember, relaxation is *re*-laxation and, each time you *re*-lax, soften your body from the top of your head to the tips of your toes. As you are doing so, you are training your body to drift off to sleep, deeper and deeper still.

Conclusion

The proverb *"An apple a day keeps the doctor away"* reflects a 19th-century belief in the health benefits of fresh fruits and vegetables—wisdom grounded in experience long before science explained why it worked. Similarly, the practices in this chapter are more than routines; they are *strategic investments* in your well-being, resilience, and leadership capacity.

Prevention is the highest and most effective form of resilience. Small, consistent actions—like integrating the *PACE Protocol* and curating a deeply personal *Bliss List*—aren't fleeting techniques. They are essential habits that form the bedrock of sustained leadership excellence.

When leaders commit to *daily autoregulation*, they don't just shield themselves from burnout and emotional ruptures—they set a powerful example. This proactive approach cultivates psychological safety, emotional stability, and collective confidence. It fosters a culture where teams feel secure, valued, and emboldened to innovate and collaborate, even in the face of adversity.

Consider this: every small moment of self-discipline compounds over time. Every intentional breath, every mental reset after a setback, and every conscious return to joy strengthens your capacity to lead with presence, clarity, and authenticity. These practices don't just prevent breakdowns—they unlock your potential to lead with greater influence and purpose.

Leading demands more than reacting well under pressure—it demands preventing stress and overwhelm from ever taking hold. In times of galloping complexity and relentless change, resilient leaders are those who actively fortify their inner world to remain steady, grounded, and adaptable.

. . .

RUPTURE PREVENTION

REMEMBER **PACE:**

- ***Permission*** lets you to lead with presence and purpose.
- ***Agency*** empowers you to override impulsive reactions.
- ***Connection*** serves as a buffer against daily stressors.
- ***Embedding*** gives you clarity, calm, and grounded confidence.

Neuro-resilience is a daily discipline. The world doesn't wait for you to feel ready—and neither should you. Let me offer a twist on an old saying:

"A practice a day keeps the Wobble away"

Begin now. Practise consistently. Refine relentlessly.

As these habits take root, you'll not only witness your personal resilience grow but also see a profound, positive shift ripple through your team and organisation.

SECTION THREE SUMMARY

This final part of 'The Inner Game' brings home the principles and importance of neuro-resilience. By focusing on the practical application of these techniques in high stakes, emotionally charged situation undergone by a real flesh-and-blood manager. Through compelling narratives and step-by-step guidance, it highlights how leaders and individuals can tackle ruptures in psychological safety, repair the damage caused by acute stress or trauma, and establish daily practices to prevent future breakdowns.

In Chapter 7: *When Safety is Ruptured*, we meet Jerry, a senior engineer in a remote mining operation whose mounting stress finally overwhelms him, leading to a complete shutdown. His "freeze" state, marked by rigidity, panic and disconnection, reveals the profound consequences of chronic stress when left unaddressed. Drawing on evolutionary biology, the chapter explains how modern day stressors activate ancient survival responses that, left to their own devices, are maladaptive in the workplace. It also explores the ripple effects of psychological safety breaches, showing how an individual's breakdown can destabilise an entire team. The chapter underscores the importance of recognising early warning signs and implementing neuro-resilience techniques to recalibrate the nervous system before stress becomes overwhelming.

Chapter 8: *Rupture Repair Coaching* builds on Jerry's story, offering a detailed account of how a skilled practitioner can help someone recover from acute stress. Through Paul's coaching session with Jerry, readers witness the power of rapport-building, humour, and neuro-resilient techniques. The session illustrates how safety priming—creating a secure emotional environment—lays the groundwork for deeper interventions. Techniques like Turning Anxiety Around and The Serenity Technique are used to reframe Jerry's internal experience, helping him transition from distress to calm, confidence, and control. The chapter demonstrates that effective coaching doesn't just resolve immediate problems but equips individuals with tools for sustained emotional self-regulation.

In Chapter 9: *Rupture Prevention*, the focus shifts from repair to prevention. Drawing on the maxim, *"An ounce of prevention is worth a pound of cure"*, the chapter explores the importance of integrating neuro-resilient routines into daily life. By adopting morning and nighttime practices, individuals can prime their bodies for calm, focus, and emotional strength while cleansing their neurology of accumulated stress. The chapter also introduces ad hoc techniques for managing difficult moments during the day and reflective rituals to address lingering negativity. These habits empower individuals to maintain psychological safety proactively, reducing the likelihood of stress spiralling into trauma.

Taken together, the chapters in this part emphasise that neuro-resilience is a dynamic process of controlling stress, recovering from disruptions, and preventing future ruptures. Leaders are shown how to create environments where psychological safety is a priority, enabling individuals and teams to thrive under pressure. Through vivid examples and actionable techniques, Elite Skills in Action provides a roadmap for transforming stress into resilience, enabling not just recovery but sustained growth and well-being.

The Inner Game Wrap Up

As you draw breath at the close of *'The Inner Game of Leadership'*, which is the first volume in the *Neuro-Resilience Skills* series, I invite you to consider not only what you've learned but also how you've learned it. This part of the book was not an arbitrary collection of insights and techniques, but a deliberately structured journey—a progression designed to mirror the very framework it seeks to teach: the PACE Protocol. From the outset, you have not merely read about *Permission, Agency, Connection* and *Embedding*; you have experienced them. The PACE Protocol has quietly guided you, not only through the content but also through the structure of the narrative itself.

Let us step back for a moment and examine this journey through the lens of the triune brain. If our brains are a layered hierarchy of evolution—reptilian at the base, mammalian in the middle, and primate (or rational) at the top—then this book has spoken to all three, engaging each in turn. At its heart, the PACE Protocol has been a tool for integration, giving each layer of the brain the opportunity to play its role in building resilience.

We began with the *Reptilian Brain*, the ancient and vigilant sentinel of survival. This part of your brain, attuned to fight, flight, and freeze, craves safety above all else. It does not ask questions or deliberate; it reacts. To soothe this primal guardian, you were offered techniques designed to bring safety into the body. Practices like the Tension Releasor and Somatic Honing whispered to the reptilian brain that the world need not always be a battlefield. The phase of *Permission* was, in many ways, a conversation with this part of you—an assurance that it could lay down its weapons, that it was, in fact, safe to explore.

From there, we ascended to the *Mammalian Brain*, home to emotion and connection. This is the brain that seeks the warmth of belonging, the comfort of co-regulation, and the vitality of social engagement. Here, Agency came into play. With the reptilian instincts dialled down, the mammalian brain could turn outward, embracing connection with the self and, by extension, others. Techniques like Wrapped in Serenity encouraged this brain to anchor itself in trust and connection, quieting the inner storms that make collaboration difficult. It was here that you began to sense not only a diminishment of survival-driven instincts but an emergence of something far greater: an increasing capacity for engagement and openness.

Finally, we spoke to the *Primate Brain*, that great architect of reason and reflection. This is the brain that delights in understanding, that seeks meaning and coherence in the patterns of life. It was engaged through logical progressions, scientific insights, and structured techniques. Decision-Journalling, for instance, allowed this part of your mind to step into the driver's seat, crafting intentional actions out of instinct and emotion. In this phase, *Connection* and *Embedding* were not abstract ideas but tangible practices, bringing the rational brain into alignment with its instinctual and emotional counterparts.

In Part Three, these ideas culminated in a focus on practical application. Through compelling narratives like Jerry's journey in a remote mining operation, we saw the profound consequences of unchecked stress and the transformative power of neuro-resilience techniques. Jerry's "freeze" state illustrated the reptilian brain in action, overwhelmed by chronic stress, and the steps taken to recover highlighted how safety priming and rapport-building could guide him toward calm and control. My coaching session with Jerry included bringing the *PACE Protocol* to life, showing how Permission, Agency, Connection, and Embedding translate into real-world leadership scenarios.

What is remarkable is that the PACE Protocol is not limited to the inner game. What you have experienced internally, as a sequence of

SECTION THREE SUMMARY

regulation and repair, will soon expand outward, shaping your interactions with others and the teams you lead. The *Permission* you gave yourself to explore will become the permission you extend to others to bring their whole selves to the table. The *Agency* you cultivated within your instincts and emotions will mirror the agency you foster within your teams. The *Connection* you cultivated within your nervous system will reflect in the trust and collaboration you create among colleagues. And the *Embedding* of new strategies, meanings and insights, which you have installed within yourself, will inspire action and momentum in the groups you guide.

This is why the PACE Protocol is not just a method; it is a philosophy. It bridges the personal and the interpersonal, the subjective and the collective, the instinctual and the intellectual. By the time you've reached this point, you have not only learned about the PACE Protocol; you have lived it. You have given your reptilian brain safety, your mammalian brain connection, and your primate brain understanding. You have aligned your inner world in preparation for the outer work that lies ahead.

As we finalise Volume I, remember this alignment. The work you've done to calm your instincts, connect with your emotions, and engage your rational mind has laid the foundation for a new kind of leadership. What began as a personal journey to conquer stress and foster resilience will now extend outward, transforming how you lead others.

In *'The Outer Game of Leadership'*, you will learn to apply the PACE Protocol to the dynamics of teams and organisations. You'll see how the emotional trust and safety you've cultivated within yourself can ripple outward, fostering a culture of resilience, adaptability, and connection within your teams. You will explore how to create environments of trust, foster meaningful connections, and align groups toward shared goals. Just as you've experienced the power of Permission, Agency, Connection, and Embedding new strategies within yourself, you will now see how these practices build resilient, unflappable teams that thrive under pressure and adapt to challenges with agility and grace.

Explored in Part Three to repair and prevent trauma:

1. **PACE Protocol** – Map and compass model for coaching
2. **PACE Yourself** – Same structure applied to self.
3. **The Bliss List** – A curated list positive experiences
4. **Rise & Shine** – Strategies for a great start to the day
5. **Get Rid of It** – Strategies for clearing out stress.
6. **Get to Sleep** – Strategies for calm restorative sleep

CONCLUSION
OWNING YOUR INNER GAME

Pause for a moment. Breathe in slowly through your nose, hold for a beat, and exhale gently. Feel the weight of your body in your chair, the tension—or lack of it—in your shoulders. Notice how your breath settles into a steady rhythm. Now, cast your mind back to the first pages of this book. How much of this awareness was present then?

Most people think of resilience as a matter of sheer willpower—a mental discipline that can be summoned when needed. But this is an illusion. Resilience is not just about how you think; it is about how your body responds under pressure. It is the difference between recognising stress and being trapped inside it.

True resilience is older than thought itself. It is not just about what you know—it is about what your body does when stress rises, when uncertainty looms, when pressure mounts. It is the difference between noticing fear and being ruled by it, between recognising instinct and being enslaved by it.

At the heart of this transformation lies your nervous system. More than anything else, this book has been an act of retraining, a slow, deliberate rewiring of the patterns that dictate your reactions to the world. It has guided you through the biology of your survival instincts, showing you not just how to regulate them, but how to harness them, refine them, and integrate them into something greater—*instinctual intelligence.*

To understand what has changed, we must look at how your nervous system has learned to shift between *Patterns of Protection* and *Patterns of Connection.* The distinction is crucial: in Patterns of Protection, your body is primed for survival—mobilised into fight or flight or immobilised into withdrawal and shutdown. Metabolically, behaviourally, and cognitively, you are in a state of defence.

But in Patterns of Connection, something else happens. The threat subsides, the nervous system signals safety, and the body shifts into an entirely different mode—one optimised for engagement, creativity, and complex thinking.

Everyone begins their neuro-resilience journey at the mercy of their nervous system—stress triggers the body, and the mind scrambles to keep up. But now, the equation has reversed. You no longer just experience stress—you shape your response to it. You are no longer a passenger; you are the driver.

Every technique, every shift, every realisation has been part of a greater biological process—one that has not only freed you from reactive survival but has given you the capacity to thrive within stress, not just endure it.

But how exactly does this rewiring occur? To see it clearly, we must turn to the three primary neural networks within your brain: the Reptilian, Mammalian, and Primate brains. As stated in Chapter 2, neuroscience confirms that the brain is far more interconnected than the Triune Brain model suggests.

Yet, like Newtonian physics, the Triune Brain model remains a simple but powerful tool. It may not capture every nuance of neural complexity, but for leaders, it offers one of the clearest ways to understand how instinct, emotion, and reason interact in real-time. It helps coaches, decision-makers, and strategists grasp the forces that drive behaviour—both in themselves and in those they lead.

To be clear, the Triune Brain Theory is a description of *neural networks*: ancient biological systems, each governing a distinct realm of experience. The fossil record shows the subtle but gradual shift from reptile to mammal to primate: so, we understand the lineage. This is confirmed by the neural networks that are present and absent in reptiles, mammals and primates today. It is certain that these three neural networks have always been present in humans.

By learning neuro-resilience skills, you have been training your three neural networks to *work together*. That means, learning to generate sufficient cues of safety to trigger a neuroception of safety within you. This is the key characteristic of a *flexible autonomic nervous system*.

The delivery mechanisms for this increased flexibility has been *Neuro-Linguistic Programming* (NLP), as I learned it from Dr. Richard Bandler and applied it as a leader and coach in commercial and non-commercial businesses for twenty-five years.

Patterns of Protection

At the base of your skull, nestled deep within the oldest structures of your brain, lies the *Reptilian Brain*. It does not care for nuance, nor for reasoned debate. It does not weigh up pros and cons, nor consider the long-term consequences of a poorly chosen word in a meeting or a rising heart rate before a difficult conversation. It is concerned with one thing alone: *survival*.

In this domain, cognition is an afterthought. When the Reptilian Brain perceives threat, it grabs the controls of your nervous system and overrides everything else. Your heartbeat quickens, your muscles tighten, and the blood drains from your frontal cortex—where higher reasoning lives—to the larger muscle groups, preparing you for fight, flight, or freeze. Your metabolism follows suit, prioritising fast-burning glucose over slower, more sustainable energy sources.

The Reptilian Brain does not plan for the future. It does not *strategise*. It does not care for connection, creativity, or even accuracy. It reacts. And yet, for all its crude simplicity, this part of your brain is also *a necessity*. Without it, you would not be here. It has saved you more times than you can count. The problem is not the existence of the Reptilian Brain—it is how often we allow it to run the show.

At the beginning of this book, much of your instinctual behaviour was governed unconsciously by these survival responses. Stressors—whether physical, emotional, or social—triggered mobilisation or immobilisation before you even had time to think. In other words, your body was responding before your mind could intervene.

You now know how to change that. Through the structured progression of techniques, you have taught your nervous system to pause, to assess, and to regulate itself before automatically defaulting to protection.

At first, this work was simple, physical, and immediate. You began with '*Somatic Honing*', learning to feel your stress responses without judgment. You used *'Tension Releaser'* and *'4-7-8 Breathing'* to signal to your body that it could exit survival mode. These were not trivial exercises; they were interventions in the very mechanics of your autonomic nervous system, ensuring *that fight, flight, and shutdown no longer dictated your experience of the world.*

And then the real shift began. You did not just *calm* the Reptilian Brain—you *trained it*. You learned to recognise its signals before they took over, mapping its sensory patterns through *'Instinct Mapping*' and building internal safety through *'Finding Home'*. Where once you were merely a passenger to its reflexes, now you are the pilot, guiding it back from mobilisation before it takes hold.

This transformation is not just psychological; it is metabolic. When you live in *chronic mobilisation*, your body burns through energy reserves faster, increasing fatigue, heightening inflammation, and impairing long-term cognitive function. Every technique you have learned has not just *relieved stress—it has optimised your body for resilience*. Your *metabolism now works with you, not against you*.

But most importantly, *your cognition has returned*. When the Reptilian Brain is in charge, deep thinking is impossible. The higher brain—the Primate Brain—receives little oxygen and less attention. If you have ever felt that stress made you 'stupid', this is why: your body quite literally redirected your mental resources elsewhere.

The change is undeniable. Now, when the Reptilian Brain activates, you *notice*. You intervene. You regulate. The survival response no longer dictates your behaviour—*it informs it*.

You are no longer merely reactive. You are responsive.

And because of this, something new has become possible. You are now capable of inhabiting the next level of resilience—the realm of connection.

Patterns of Connection

If the Reptilian Brain is the body's emergency response system, then the Mammalian Brain—the limbic system—is its emotional compass. This is where the world is no longer a question of survival, but of meaning, memory, and connection. It is here that stress ceases to be merely metabolic and becomes something personal.

For the Mammalian Brain, safety is not just the absence of threat—it is *the presence of trust, warmth, and social belonging*. And yet, when the body is locked in survival mode, these things feel distant, if not impossible. A nervous system trapped in a *Pattern of Protection* cannot fully engage in *Patterns of Connection*. It cannot think freely, love freely, or lead freely. It remains on edge, mistaking colleagues for competitors, mistakes for disasters, challenges for threats. It is not the external world that has changed—*only the internal conditions of the nervous system.*

Throughout this book, you have gradually shifted these internal conditions. At first, the Mammalian Brain, conditioned by past experiences, resisted the idea that safety could be created rather than passively experienced. Emotional states, after all, had long felt like something that happened to you, rather than something you could shape. But as your Reptilian Brain became regulated, your Mammalian Brain became free to do something it could not before: experience safety fully.

This was not a matter of wishful thinking, nor of mere emotional management. It was biological. Through *'Finding Home'*, you built neural associations between calmness and stability, rather than calmness and waiting for the next disaster. With *'Bliss List'*, you trained your nervous system to access joy on command, proving that positivity is not a passive state but an active skill. With *'Silencing the Storm'*, you rewired the circuits that once turned minor stressors into looping, inescapable ruminations.

But the greatest transformation was in how you now relate to others.

The limbic system is not designed for isolation. It is wired for co-regulation, meaning that its *default state is shaped not just by your own nervous system, but by those around you.* You now recognise this intuitively. You have seen how tension spreads through a room like electricity. You have felt the difference between a voice that soothes and a voice that sharpens. You have noticed that *safety is a social phenomenon, not just an individual one.*

The question, then, was never just whether you could regulate yourself, but whether you could *regulate others through your presence, your voice, and your leadership.*

CONCLUSION

You read how I used *Safety Priming* and *Co-Regulating Humour* could be used in the process of repairing trauma. You will learn about these explicitly in 'The Outer Game of Leadership'. Safety, you discovered, is not just a personal feeling, but an interaction your nervous system is having with the environment. You learned to soften stress in conversations before it took hold. You recognised that the way you present yourself—your tone, your facial expressions, your openness—actively dictates whether those around you remain in protection or shift into connection.

And this can change everything.

Leadership, decision-making, and problem-solving can all improve—not because you learned new intellectual skills, but because you have learned to keep yourself in the optimal state for thinking. What once was personal resilience is now something broader, something more fundamental: social fluency, the ability to lead not just with authority, but with presence, trust, and psychological safety.

The Mammalian Brain, once ruled by stress, is now ruled by awareness. You know how to recognise when your own nervous system is slipping into protection, and just as importantly, you now recognise it in others. You see when a colleague's frustration is really fear. You sense when a team member's withdrawal is not laziness, but immobilisation. And most importantly, you know what to do about it.

This is not just resilience—it is *leadership over the social nervous system*.

And because of this, a new possibility opens: not just controlling emotions, but controlling the conditions under which collective thinking flourishes.

To understand this final transformation, we must turn to the Primate Brain—the seat of logic, reason, and innovation. The place where cognition is either *trapped by stress or liberated by safety*.

Cognitive Overload

There is a persistent illusion, deeply embedded in contemporary thought, that reason operates separately from emotion—that clear, rational thinking is a purely intellectual exercise, rising above the turbulence of the body. But this is a fantasy. A mind in distress is a mind in disarray. The Primate Brain—the neocortex, our seat of logic, strategy, and foresight—is not an autonomous command centre. It is a dependent system, entirely contingent on the conditions of the nervous system beneath it.

No matter how intelligent a person is, when their body is locked in survival mode, higher reasoning is off the table. Stress hijacks cognition, diverting resources away from deep thought and long-term planning into immediate, reactive decision-making. The more the body perceives threat, the less the mind can engage in what we associate with true intelligence: creativity, strategic foresight, and the ability to weigh consequences beyond the immediate moment.

This is why what is often called 'poor decision-making' is, at its core, not a failure of intelligence—but a failure of state. It is not that people become irrational under pressure; it is that their cognitive bandwidth shrinks, compressed by the body's demand for survival. A leader caught in a state of stress does not simply think worse—they think differently, trapped in a survival triage: fight, flee, or freeze.

At the start of this book, your Primate Brain was often working against itself. When stress arose, it followed the path it had always followed: over-analysing, spiralling into worry, cycling through worst-case scenarios. It tried to solve emotions with logic—like attempting to put out a fire by reading about water. You knew you were 'overthinking', but knowing was not enough to stop it. You had no mechanism for interrupting the momentum of cognitive overload before it consumed you.

CONCLUSION

But cognition is not an isolated process—it is a state-dependent phenomenon. The quality of your thinking is not dictated by willpower or intellect, but by whether your nervous system is in a state where complex thought is possible.

This is the crucial shift. Instead of trying to fix thinking directly, you learned to shift the conditions under which clear thinking emerges.

At first, this involved simple but powerful interventions.

- *Dual-Mind Reflection* allowed your rational mind to engage with your instincts rather than dismiss them.
- *The Worry Solver* reframed stress into action, preventing rumination from spiralling into paralysis.
- *Stepping Out of Fear* allowed your neocortex the space to function without the weight of emotional overwhelm.

And then, as the Mammalian Brain settled into safety, something even more profound happened: thinking became effortless. No longer tangled in a constant battle against stress, your Primate Brain could return to its full capacity—fluid, agile, sharp.

This cannot be overstated: cognition is not just something to be improved—it is something to be transformed. It has already begun.

- You no longer waste mental energy on unnecessary overanalyses, because you now recognise the difference between useful thought and stress-driven mental noise.
- You no longer burn hours wrestling with decisions, because you trust your instincts to signal what requires attention and what does not.
- Most importantly, your nervous system has been rewired so that under pressure, your thinking does not degrade—it sharpens.

This is what instinctual intelligence truly means. It is not merely the ability to regulate emotions, nor is it simply the capacity to think clearly under stress. It is something greater: the full integration of survival, emotion, and intellect into a seamless whole—where instinct does not overpower thought, and thought does not ignore instinct.

It is the ability to move fluidly between mobilisation, connection, and cognition—to detect, understand, and shape the shifting patterns of your nervous system, so that in any given moment, you are operating from the most effective state possible.

For the first time:

- Your Reptilian Brain does not react blindly—it signals usefully.
- Your Mammalian Brain does not overwhelm you with emotion—it informs you.
- Your Primate Brain does not collapse under stress—it remains clear, sharp, and adaptive.

And this, ultimately, is the mark of true resilience.

Not merely the ability to withstand hardship, but the ability to navigate complexity with intelligence, presence, and control.

- Where once survival ruled, now modern humans can flourish.
- Where once protection dictated action, now connection and cognition can coexist.

This is not just a new way of managing stress.

This is a new way of *being*.

True Instinctual Intelligence

CONCLUSION

The mind does not work in isolation. The sharpest intellect in the world is useless when the nervous system is dysregulated. And yet, most leaders attempt to solve stress-driven thinking failures by thinking harder. They push through, unaware that they are battling their own biology.

True intelligence is not found in forcing reason to overcome instinct—it is found in integrating the two. This is where instinctual intelligence begins.

Neuro-resilience is not about willpower; it is about rewiring the nervous system. At the start of this journey, your mind and body were pulling in different directions.

- The Reptilian Brain, ever-vigilant, triggered fight, flight, or freeze at the first sign of stress, flooding your system with adrenaline before your conscious mind could even process what was happening.
- The Mammalian Brain, shaped by past experiences, reacted emotionally—sometimes protecting, sometimes connecting, but often reinforcing old habits of fear, withdrawal, or overstimulation.
- The Primate Brain, the grand architect of reason, tried to impose order, attempting to think its way out of stress while unknowingly making the situation worse.

This constant internal struggle—the overthinking, the emotional highs and lows, the inexplicable anxiety that rises unbidden—is what most people consider normal. The human condition. The exhaustion of a nervous system that never seems fully at ease. No wonder so many live in a perpetual state of mental and emotional depletion, their bodies locked in Patterns of Protection long after the threats have passed.

But now, the conflict has begun to resolve. Something fundamental has shifted.

When your three brains move out of sync, you now have the ability to realign them.

- Where once your instincts hijacked you, they now act as early-warning signals—alerting you to stress without overwhelming you.
- Where once your emotions dictated your behaviour, they now serve as tools for insight, motivation, and connection.
- And where once your rational mind fought against stress, it is now free to think, plan, and lead with clarity.

This is instinctual intelligence—a state where all parts of the system work together, where protection no longer overrides connection, and cognition is no longer derailed by emotion. But what, exactly, has changed?

At a physiological level, you have built flexibility into your autonomic nervous system. Your body, once primed for habitual stress responses, now knows how to shift into a state of regulation deliberately. What was once disruptive—fight, flight, freeze—has now become adaptive, a response that is chosen rather than imposed. This means that under pressure, instead of collapsing into a survival state, your system remains fluid and responsive. You do not lose yourself in stress—you remain present.

At an emotional level, you have learned to trust the signals of your body rather than fear them. What once felt like chaos—anxiety, uncertainty, physiological discomfort—is now understood as information, a message from your nervous system rather than an enemy to be fought. And this trust has allowed you to access a new kind of control —not the rigid suppression of emotions, but the fluid, dynamic control of mastery. And cognitively? The greatest transformation of all.

You have discovered what few ever do: that the brain works best when it is not at war with itself. That intelligence is not just about knowledge, but about state—the ability to maintain the conditions in which thinking is sharpest, creativity is at its peak, and decisions are made not from fear, but from clarity.

This is not just a different way of processing stress. It is a different way of being. From this moment forward, resilience is not something you do. It is something you are. It is woven into the structure of your nervous system, embedded in your responses, present in the very way you hold yourself, breathe, speak, and lead. Your body knows safety. Your mind knows control. Your instincts, once erratic, now serve you. You have, at last, become fully integrated.

And from here, anything is possible.

The Wind Beneath the Wings

If this journey has felt fluid, if each step seemed to unfold naturally from the last, if the transformation you have begun to experience has felt unforced and inevitable—it is because Volume I was more than just a collection of scientific theories and fact combined with a series of matching NLP insights and strategies. Rather, it was a carefully structured process.

Every chapter, every exercise, every realisation was selected to follow the same rhythm that governs all successful change: first, creating trust and safety, then cultivating personal control, then deepening social fluency, and finally installing strategies and meanings for the long-term. This is not coincidence—it is the structure that allows resilience to move from theory into instinct, from knowledge into lived intelligence.

The PACE Protocol is not just a framework that was presented and explained to you. It is the method that was applied to the structure of Volume I to support your cognitive, emotional and instinctual journey of learning. It was the unseen framework that has made everything feel more intuitive and more digestible towards being, more lasting.

You will not have just surfed atop of the process—you will have experienced it with the *Primate, Mammalian* and *Reptile* brains. This is to say that you have been learning both consciously (slow-thinking) and unconsciously (fast-thinking). The same structure that had begun to rewire your nervous system over these pages is now an embedded learning within you.

With continued practice, which builds up the unconscious competence of the fast-thinking system, resilience will begin to feel like 'a part of who you are and just do', rather than something you must 'remember to apply'. That is why it's 'neuro-resilience' and what you have been practicing are 'neuro-resilience skills'. So, let's now touch on some practice.

Neuro-Resilience is Practiced Skills

Resilience is not an achievement. It is not a trophy to be placed on a shelf, nor a finish line to be crossed with a sigh of relief. It is a set of skills that must be practiced. Resilience is not a one-time achievement. It is an ongoing interaction between your nervous system and your environment. Without continued engagement, even the sharpest instincts dull.

The mistake many make is assuming that transformation is permanent simply because it has been experienced once. They assume that because they have felt clarity, they will always think clearly. Because they have found calm, they will always remain calm. But the nervous system is not a machine—it does not retain new habits through willpower alone. It is an adaptive, living system, shaped by what it is repeatedly exposed to. *What you reinforce is what remains.* That is why the work does not end here.

The skills you have gained, the instincts you have rewired, the clarity you now possess—these are *not fixed traits but cultivated conditions.* They exist because you have trained them into being. And they will remain, not because you understand them, but because you *continue to practise them.*

Neuro-Resilience Daily Routine

These three daily practices are not rigid formulas but adaptable frameworks that evolve as you refine what works best for you. As with any skill, leadership resilience is built through *purposeful practice—*tweaking, testing, and noodling with different approaches until they become second nature. Over time, you'll learn to *do the little things better and really well,* making these habits more fluid and effective. What follows is a great place to start that pursuit of *perfect practice.*

1. 'Rise & Shine'

Start your day ready to be the best version of yourself. Mornings set the stage for the entire day, so the *Rise & Shine* practice ensures you begin with energy, clarity, and intention. Start with controlled *breathing—*if you need an energy boost, use *Box Breathing* (inhale for four, hold for four, exhale for four). If you wake up anxious, try *4-7-8 Breathing* to regulate your nervous system.

Next, engage with your *Bliss List—*whether you need an *energiser* (vividly reliving triumphant, joyful, or playful moments) or a *calmer* (recalling serene, grounding experiences). Use sensory detail to make the memory immersive. Once you've primed your state, move into *PACE Yourself:*

- *Permission* – Have you permitted yourself to lead well confidently?

- *Agency* – Are your actions the best blends of reason and instinct?
- *Connection* – Are you spinning a good feeling and socially engaged?
- *Embedding* – Have you pre-lived and pre-framed any challenges ahead?

By the time you've finished this process, you've already won the morning—you are stepping into the day as the best leader you can be.

2. 'Get Rid of It'

Throughout the day, stress, frustrations, peeves and, in the modern vernacular, 'micro-aggressions' can and do build up. If left unchecked, these accumulate, leading to disengagement, irritability, or exhaustion.

The *Get Rid of It* practice is about *taking out the garbage*—processing and releasing emotional tension before it festers. Start by mentally scanning your day for any unresolved stressors.

Then, use a structured *leadership hygiene practice* to clear them:

- *Flicker the Image* – Take any stressful memory, make it black and white, and flicker it rapidly for five counts.
- *Shrink the Image* – Push it away until it becomes tiny. Repeat five times.
- *Rewind the Memory* – Play the experience backward with all the sounds and movements reversed.

By shifting these VAK *submodalities*, you break the emotional grip of the stressor, allowing your body to reset. Just as you wouldn't let dirty dishes pile up in the sink, don't let stress accumulate in your mind—clear it daily to stay sharp, connected, and adaptable. Practice makes perfect and perfection is lots of little things done well. In NLP, those 'little things' almost always involve ways to shift submodalities.

3. 'Get to Sleep'

The *Get to Sleep* practice ensures that you don't carry the day's stress into the night. Sleep is your body's most powerful recovery tool, but poor mental habits—such as replaying anxieties or running worst-case scenarios—can sabotage it. Begin with *breathing* to shift into relaxation mode. If your mind is racing, return to *4-7-8 breathing* or a slow, deep diaphragmatic rhythm. Then, engage with your *Bliss List*, selecting calming experiences that bring you into a state of gentle joy —soothing music, a warm breeze, the sound of laughter. Immerse yourself in these memories using soft internal dialogue to deepen relaxation. If sleep disruptions occur, don't fight them—gently return to your *Bliss List* and re-lax multiple times, allowing your body to associate bedtime with peace and safety. Sleep is the ultimate integration process. Guard it fiercely.

Integrated Intelligence for Life

You began this journey reacting. You end it responding proactively. You began ruled by instincts operating below your conscious control. Now you can end in command of it.

But resilience is not something you hold onto—it is something you practise, something you embody, something that is *only as strong as the habits that sustain it*.

This is your work now. To maintain what you have built. To sharpen what you have cultivated. To carry this not just as knowledge, but as a way of being.

And if ever you find yourself slipping, losing clarity, feeling the return of old patterns, that's your body telling you it is sensing something. Maybe it's receiving a true signal. Maybe it's wrongly sensing noise. Remember:

- If your body's survival mode reflects your environment, in that you are in real and imminent danger or life threat, immediately take the necessary action to get physically safe. Emotional safety will return once your body senses it is safe.

- If your body is out of sync with your environment, in that you are <u>not</u> in actual danger: hey, shit happens! We're not infallible and we have to live in this uncertain and ambiguous reality. You've just been blown off course, but you've got the skillset. Get your body's metabolism back in sync with your actual environment.

How do you do that? Tune your cognition back into your instincts—do the *Worry Solver*, the *Dual-Mind Reflection*, *Stepping Out of Fear*, *Turn Anxiety Around*, *Get Rid of It* and get *Wrapped in Serenity*.

You have already rewired your nervous system. The intelligence, the control, the instinctive ability—they are all still there. You need only return to them. This is your path now.

Resilience is not theory. Resilience is practice. Resilience is a state of activation—the more you engage with it, the stronger it becomes. This is more than just everyday resilience—it is full command over the conditions of your intelligence. The future no longer dictates your course—you shape it, moment by moment. This is *neuro-resilience*.

AFTERWORD
THE LEADER YOU HAVE BECOME

There comes a point in every leader's life—not with a crash, but with a quiet shift—when the noise outside finally loses its grip. The emails can wait. The pressure no longer grips the chest. The inner voice, the one so often buried beneath urgency and performance, begins to speak in a tone that is steady. Familiar. Yours.

You've felt it, haven't you? The subtle difference between reacting and responding. The pause before the outburst. The breath that steadies your hand when everything around you is shaking. That moment wasn't luck. It was skill. Trained, not born.

If you've come this far, then you haven't just read this book—you've trained through it. You've touched the edges of your nervous system and brought it back into your command. You've witnessed the tide of your instinct rise and chosen not to be swept away. That's not just progress. That's leadership.

Resilience is often sold as toughness. But the kind of resilience you've cultivated here isn't rigid. It bends. It breathes. It listens before it speaks. It absorbs without collapsing. It sees clearly—even in the fog of stress—and acts not from panic but from presence.

There was a time when stress may have felt like an adversary. When instincts betrayed you, and self-regulation felt out of reach. When leadership was a performance—tight shoulders, steady voice, trying to appear unshakeable while something trembled just beneath the surface.

But not now. Now you meet your inner signals like an old companion. You don't suppress them; you listen. You don't deny the pressure; you let it move through. You've shifted from suppressing your state to shaping it—from fearing your instincts to refining them. What was once reactive has become deliberate.

This shift is not cosmetic. It is foundational. You've strengthened the fibre of your nervous system. You've rehearsed new habits of breath, attention, and internal recovery. And those habits are what make you trustworthy—not just to others, but to yourself.

Still, this is not the end of the work. Inner mastery is never final. You will face meetings that unsettle, conflicts that rattle, decisions that strain your clarity. But now, you meet those moments with something rare: self-possession. The capacity to return to yourself, again and again, no matter what the world demands.

Picture yourself in one of those moments—where voices rise, the stakes climb, and the room leans into fear. Feel your feet on the floor. The breath in your chest. The stillness you carry, not as an act but as a state. Others may not name it, but they'll feel it. That calm presence will become your leadership signature.

So take a moment. Reflect. Not on how far you still have to go, but how far you've already come. Remember who you were when you first opened these pages. That version of you was already capable—just not yet trained. And now? You are the same person, only steadier. Clearer. Ready.

This is your foundation. The outer game will build on it—but it is here, in the stillness beneath the storm, where true leadership begins.

Lead from within. The rest will follow.

Paul O'Neill

November 2024

NOTES

1. INSTINCTUAL CONTACT

1. MacLean, P. D. (1990). *The triune brain in evolution: Role in paleocerebral functions.* Springer.
2. The enteric nervous system (ENS) is often referred to as the 'second brain' due to its extensive network of neurons in the gut. See: Gershon, M.D. (1998). *The Second Brain: A Groundbreaking New Understanding of Nervous Disorders of the Stomach and Intestine*; and
    Damasio, A. R. (1994). *Descartes' error: Emotion, reason and the human brain.* Putnam.
3. Freud, S. (1915/2001). *The unconscious.* In *The standard edition of the complete psychological works of Sigmund Freud*(Vol. 14). Vintage.
4. The gut-brain axis involves a bidirectional communication network between the central and enteric nervous systems. This interaction significantly affects emotional regulation and cognitive functioning under stress.
5. This emphasis on integrating instinct and cognition reflects themes from Gigerenzer's research on heuristics and intuitive intelligence. See: Gigerenzer, G. (2007). *Gut Feelings: The Intelligence of the Unconscious.*

2. INSTINCTUAL AWARENESS

1. MacLean, P. D. (1990). *The Triune Brain in Evolution: Role in Paleocerebral Functions.* This theory posits that the human brain evolved in three major parts: reptilian (survival), limbic (emotion), and neocortex (reason).
2. MacLean, P. D. (1990). *The triune brain in evolution: Role in paleocerebral functions.* Springer.
3. The 'fight, flight, or freeze' response is part of the autonomic nervous system's defence mechanism, originally mapped by Walter Cannon and later refined in trauma studies by Peter Levine and Bessel van der Kolk.
4. While the Triune Brain model is debated in modern neuroscience, it remains a useful metaphor for explaining instinctive reactions, especially in leadership and coaching contexts
5. Kahneman, D. (2011). *Thinking, fast and slow.* Farrar, Straus and Giroux.

3. INSTINCTUAL ACUITY

1. Porges, S. W. (2011). *The Polyvagal Theory: Neurophysiological Foundations of*

Emotions, Attachment, Communication, and Self-Regulation. Neuroception refers to the body's unconscious system for detecting safety, danger, or life threat.
2. This technique draws on NLP reframing strategies and pattern detection, pioneered by Richard Bandler, which treat worry as a signal from the unconscious that can be reframed and redeployed. See Bandler, R. (1985). *Using Your Brain—for a Change*.
3. van der Kolk, B. (2014). *The body keeps the score: Brain, mind and body in the healing of trauma*. Viking.
4. This story is cited by Porges as an example of neuroception in action: an embodied form of unconscious safety detection critical to survival, even without logical reasoning
5. Richard Bandler, co-creator of Neuro-Linguistic Programming (NLP), has written extensively on pattern recognition, submodalities, and altering state through reframing.
    See: Bandler, R. (2008). *Get the Life You Want*.
6. The Unconscious Navigator concept resonates with Daniel Kahneman's System 1 (fast, intuitive) thinking. See: Kahneman, D. (2011). *Thinking, Fast and Slow*.
7. Bandler, R. (1985). *Using your brain for a change: Neuro-linguistic programming*. Real People Press.
8. This process uses kinaesthetic anchoring and memory amplification techniques developed in Neuro-Linguistic Programming (NLP), particularly Bandler's emphasis on shifting emotional states through vivid mental rehearsal and body-based focus. See Bandler, R. & Andreas, S. (1987). *Using Your Brain—for a Change*.

INTRODUCTION

1. This metaphor parallels the concept of self-regulation as dynamic steering—central to emotional intelligence frameworks. See Goleman, D. (1995). *Emotional Intelligence*.
2. The notion that modern stress responses are rooted in ancient neurological circuits is central to Polyvagal Theory. See Porges, S. (2011). *The Polyvagal Theory: Neurophysiological Foundations of Emotions, Attachment, Communication, and Self-regulation*.

4. CORE SKILLS

1. Jacques Lecoq (1921–1999) was a French actor and movement coach who developed a widely respected approach to physical theatre, based on body awareness and instinctive action.
2. This notion draws on the evolutionary continuity between species, notably articulated in Charles Darwin's *The Descent of Man* (1871), where he argued that humans retain the physical and behavioural residues of their ancestral past.
3. Instinct Mapping is influenced by NLP submodality techniques, which explore

NOTES   199

how sensory details structure internal experience. See Bandler, R. & MacDonald, W. (1988). *An Insider's Guide to Submodalities*.

5. INTERMEDIATE SKILLS

1. This technique builds on cognitive distancing and visual dissociation strategies found in NLP and trauma therapy. See Bandler, R. & Grinder, J. (1979). *Frogs Into Princes*.
2. *This technique draws directly on Richard Bandler's work with submodality shifts and timeline reframing in Neuro-Linguistic Programming (NLP), used to change the emotional charge of painful memories.* See Bandler, R. (1985). *Using Your Brain—for a Change*.
    *It also echoes findings from trauma studies on memory reconsolidation and embodied trauma.
    Reframing emotional memory content draws from memory reconsolidation research and trauma reframing approaches. See van der Kolk, B. (2014). *The Body Keeps the Score*.
3. This inner dialogue restructuring method is derived from Bandler's pattern interruption techniques and the NLP "Meta Model," which deconstructs limiting language patterns. See Bandler, R. & Grinder, J. (1975). *The Structure of Magic, Vol. 1*.
    It also has parallels in narrative therapy that encourage the re-authoring of internal stories. See White, M. & Epston, D. (1990). *Narrative Means to Therapeutic Ends*.

6. ADVANCED SKILLS

1. *This method of noticing the "spin" of anxiety and reversing it draws from Richard Bandler's "Neuro-Hypnotic Repatterning" (NHR), a technique that builds on submodality directionality to collapse or overwrite emotional patterns. See Bandler, R. (2008). *Get the Life You Want: The Secrets to Quick and Lasting Life Change*.
2. Bandler, R. (2008). *Get the life you want: The secrets to quick and lasting life change with neuro-linguistic programming*. Health Communications.

SECTION TWO SUMMARY

1. This concept aligns with somatic psychology, which posits that the body often initiates responses before conscious cognition. See Levine, P. (1997). *Waking the Tiger: Healing Trauma*.
2. These techniques aim to restore and optimise the 'window of tolerance'—the zone of optimal arousal for functioning. See Siegel, D. (2012). *The Developing Mind*.

7. WHEN SAFETY IS RUPTURED

1. The 'freeze' response is a survival mechanism governed by the dorsal vagal system, part of the Polyvagal Theory introduced by Stephen Porges
2. MacLean, P. D. (1990). *The Triune Brain in Evolution*. This framework describes the layered structure of human emotion, with survival instincts driven by the 'reptilian brain'
3. Richard Bandler. Often used in stress-management workshops to emphasise neuroplasticity and mindset choice

8. RUPTURE REPAIR COACHING

1. Bandler, R. (2008). *Get the life you want: The secrets to quick and lasting life change with neuro-linguistic programming*. Health Communications Inc.
2. This culinary metaphor illustrates neuroplastic coaching: just as chefs manipulate ingredients to affect biology, skilled coaches shape subjective experience to shift emotional and physiological states
3. The PACE Protocol (Prime, Agency, Connect, Embed) draws inspiration from Richard Bandler's live demonstrations—particularly his work on emotional pacing and layered anchoring, as seen in his *Konstanz* DVD. The structure integrates NLP's pacing techniques with trauma-informed coaching, offering a fluid framework for regulating emotional states and re-patterning behavioural responses.

BIBLIOGRAPHY

Books

Aristotle. (2009). *The Nicomachean ethics* (W. D. Ross, Trans.). Oxford University Press. (Original work c. 4th century BCE)

Bandler, R. (1985). *Using your brain for a change: Neuro-linguistic programming*. Real People Press.

Bandler, R. (2008). *Get the life you want: The secrets to quick and lasting life change with neuro-linguistic programming*. Health Communications.

Bandler, R., & Grinder, J. (1975). *The structure of magic I: A book about language and therapy*. Science and Behavior Books.

Bandler, R., & Grinder, J. (1979). *Frogs into princes: Neuro linguistic programming*. Real People Press.

Damasio, A. R. (1994). *Descartes' error: Emotion, reason and the human brain*. Putnam.

Damasio, A. R. (1999). *The feeling of what happens: Body, emotion and the making of consciousness*. Heinemann.

Dana, D. (2018). *The polyvagal theory in therapy: Engaging the rhythm of regulation*. W. W. Norton.

Darwin, C. (1871). *The descent of man, and selection in relation to sex*. John Murray.

Dawkins, R. (1976). *The selfish gene*. Oxford University Press.

Dawkins, R. (1982). *The extended phenotype: The long reach of the gene*. Oxford University Press.

Dawkins, R. (2006). *The God delusion*. Bantam Press.

Dennett, D. C. (1991). *Consciousness explained*. Little, Brown and Company.

Dennett, D. C. (1995). *Darwin's dangerous idea: Evolution and the meanings of life*. Simon & Schuster.

Dennett, D. C. (2003). *Freedom evolves*. Penguin Books.

Edmondson, A. C. (2018). *The fearless organisation: Creating psychological safety in the workplace for learning, innovation, and growth*. Wiley.

Franklin, B. (n.d.). *Poor Richard's almanack*. (Quoted aphorism: "An ounce of prevention is worth a pound of cure.")

Freud, S. (1915/2001). The unconscious. In J. Strachey (Ed. & Trans.), *The standard edition of the complete psychological works of Sigmund Freud* (Vol. 14, pp. 159–215). Vintage. (Original work published 1915)

Goffman, E. (1959). *The presentation of self in everyday life*. Anchor Books.

Goleman, D. (1995). *Emotional intelligence: Why it can matter more than IQ*. Bantam Books.

Huxley, A. (1965). *Island*. Chatto & Windus.

Jacobs, B. (2014). *The embodied leader: A somatic approach to developing your leadership*. Jossey-Bass.

Kahneman, D. (2011). *Thinking, fast and slow*. Farrar, Straus and Giroux.

LeDoux, J. (1996). *The emotional brain: The mysterious underpinnings of emotional life*. Simon & Schuster.

Levine, P. A. (1997). *Waking the tiger: Healing trauma*. North Atlantic Books.

MacLean, P. D. (1990). *The triune brain in evolution: Role in paleocerebral functions*. Springer.

Mandela, N. (1994). *Long walk to freedom: The autobiography of Nelson Mandela*. Little, Brown and Company.

McKenna, P. (2009). *Control stress: Stop worrying and feel good now!*. Bantam Press.

McKenna, P. (2017). *Freedom from anxiety*. Hay House.

McKenna, P. (2010). *I can make you confident*. Sterling Publishing.

Orwell, G. (1949). *Nineteen eighty-four*. Secker & Warburg.

Porges, S. W. (2011). *The polyvagal theory: Neurophysiological foundations of emotions, attachment, communication, and self-regulation*. W. W. Norton.

Rowling, J. K. (2008). *The tales of Beedle the Bard*. Bloomsbury.

Siegel, D. J. (2010). *The mindful therapist: A clinician's guide to mindsight and neural integration*. W. W. Norton.

Sun Tzu. (2009). *The art of war* (L. Giles, Trans.). Arcturus Publishing. (Original work c. 5th century BCE)

Sutton, R. I. (2007). *The no asshole rule: Building a civilised workplace and surviving one that isn't*. Business Plus.

van der Kolk, B. A. (2014). *The body keeps the score: Brain, mind and body in the healing of trauma*. Viking.

White, M. P. (1990). *White heat*. Ebury Press.

Zhuangzi. (2009). *Zhuangzi: Basic writings* (B. Watson, Trans.). Columbia University Press. (Original work c. 4th century BCE)

Zinsser, W. (2006). *On writing well: The classic guide to writing nonfiction* (30th anniversary ed.). Harper Perennial.

Audio/CD Recordings

Bandler, R. (2000). *Soften Too!* [Audio CD]. Excellence Quest Training International.

Bandler, R. (2003). *Medicine Show* [CD set]. Business NLP Ltd.

Bandler, R. (2011). *Persuasion Engineering* [CD set]. NLP Life Training.

McKenna, P. (2022). *Positivity* [Audio program]. Audible Originals.

McKenna, P., & Breen, M. (1998). *The power to influence* [Audio recording]. Nightingale-Conant.

Video/DVD Recordings

Bandler, R. (1992). The adventures of anybody [Video]. NLP Comprehensive.

Bandler, R. (1993). Anxiety relief and phobia cure [Video]. NLP Seminars Group International.

Bandler, R. (1994). Personal enhancement series [DVD series]. NLP Comprehensive.
Bandler, R. (2002). Trance-formations live [DVD]. NLP Life Training.
Bandler, R. (2004). Richard Bandler in Konstanz: Advanced NLP Seminar [DVD]. NLP Life Training / NLP Seminars Group International.

INDEX
(TOOLS, TECHNIQUES & SKILLS IN BOLD AND ITALICS)

Anchor(ing): 65–67, 145, 168,
Aristotle: 147
Breathing:

- ***4-7-8 Breathing***: 22, 29, 187
- ***Box Breathing***: 153, 185

Congruence, metabolic: 4, 39
Connect with Yourself: 36, 50
Daniel Kahneman: 20
Decision Journaling: 32-35, 48
Finding Home: 66-68, 97
Future Pacing: 145
Gazelle (metaphor): 55, 59–60
Get Rid of It: 156–159, 186
Get to Sleep: 159–162, 187
Immobilisation: 55–59, 112, 172–177
Instinct Mapping: 62, 94
Jerry: 111–119, 128–146
Joy light: 36
Mobilisation: 55–59, 112, 172–177
Neuroception: 4, 26–31, 128
Neuro-Hypnotic Repatterning (NHR): 82
Neuro-Linguistic Programing (NLP): 56, 61, 82, 123–128, 148
PACE Protocol: 124–127
PACE Yourself: 148–150
Polyvagal Theory: 26–28
Primate Brain: 4, 13–16, 20–29, 70–71
Psychological safety: 11, 57, 108–119, 148, 163
Reptilian Brain: 4, 11–16, 20–29, 70–71
Richard Bandler: 32, 36, 62, 82, 83, 113–115, 121–125, 159
Rise & Shine: 153–156, 185
Safety Priming: 131–145
Safety Rupture: 121–165
Sarah: 152
Sharon: 8–15, 19, 26–27, 67
Silencing the Storm: 78–79,
Social engagement: 15, 56, 112, 128, 150

Somatic Honing: 53, 195
Stephen Porges: 26-28
Stepping Out of Fear: 71–73, 99
Submodalities: 61–64, 86–88, 94–96, 145–148, 158
Taming Vicious Memories: 74–76, 100
Tension Releasor: 16–18, 43
Bliss List: 150–152
Triune Brain: 4, 13–15
Turning Anxiety Around: 83–87
Worry Solver: 28–29
Wrapped in Serenity: 87–89
Zhuangzi: 111

ACKNOWLEDGMENTS

My sincere thanks to **Francinne Kaye Gacilo**, whose sharp eye and creative mind brought this book to life in more ways than one.

As a digital media specialist with a flair for graphic design, Francinne not only proofread the manuscript with care but also contributed a series of interior graphics that added clarity, elegance, and visual depth to the pages.

Her work helped turn concepts into compelling visuals, and for that, I'm deeply grateful.

ABOUT THE AUTHOR

Paul O'Neill is trusted by professionals in business, heavy industry, medical and mental health, and elite sports as consultant, coach and guide. For more than twenty-five years, he's been doing exactly that: guiding individuals, teams and entire organisations through the thickets of change, chaos and contradiction with a calm intensity that refuses to settle for surface solutions.

His leadership record spans continents and industries, yet his work never follows a formula. That's the point. Real transformation, he insists, can't be imposed or standardised. It must be built, brick by deliberate brick, in the language, rhythm, and logic of those who live it.

Clients across Australia, New Zealand, the UK, North America, and South Africa describe him as 'visionary', 'invaluable', 'a lifelong friend' - though the word most often repeated is 'transformational'. Not because Paul performs miracles, but because he hands the tools over. He trains people to recognise patterns, to respond to pressure with composure, to build resilience that sticks - not just in the individual nervous system, but in the culture of entire teams.

Paul's training and coaching in neuro-resilience skills, verbal and non-verbal skills, group dynamics, complex problem-solving, stakeholder engagement and adaptive strategic leadership has helped professionals across sectors rewrite their stories - by both negating the harsh effect change can have on the leaders, as well as by navigating their group through it differently. He's known for making the complex understandable, for challenging the status quo with warmth and rigour, and for turning the work of change into something deeply human and fiercely practical.

He remains, above all else, a practitioner. Someone who steps in, shoulder to shoulder, as a guide; and he stays until the work is done.

If you've reached the edge of what you know and understand, Paul is someone you want in the room.

ALSO BY PAUL O'NEILL

Neuro-Resilience Skills
Volume I: The Inner Game of Leadership:
Volume II: The Outer Game of Leadership

Six Pillars of Successful Executives
Pillar 1: Personal Resilience

Pillar 2: Non-Verbal Cues

Pillar 3: Pristine Problem Solving

Pillar 4: Impactful Speaking

Pillar 5: Engagement Excellence

Pillar 6: Strategic Resilience

NLP Mastery for Leaders
1. Neuro: Adapted Wisdoms

2. Linguistic: Language & Logic

3. Programming: Moving as One